INDESCRIBABLE ATLAS ADVENTURES

WITH 50+ MAPS!

AN EXPLORER'S GUIDE TO GEOGRAPHY, ANIMALS, AND CULTURES THROUGH GOD'S AMAZING WORLD

LOUIE GIGLIO

ILLUSTRATED BY NICOLA ANDERSON
& LYNSEY WILSON

An Imprint of Thomas Nelson

CONTENTS

EXPLORE THE WORLD
- INTRODUCTION 4
- WORLD MAP 6
- NORTH AMERICA 8
- SOUTH AMERICA 20
- AFRICA 36
- EUROPE 52
- ASIA 72
- AUSTRALIA AND OCEANIA 98
- POLAR REGIONS 104
- INDEX 110

CANADA 10
UNITED STATES 12
MEXICO 14
COSTA RICA 16
CUBA 18
VENEZUELA 24
COLOMBIA 22
PERU 26
AMAZON RAINFOREST 30
BRAZIL 28
CHILE 32
ARGENTINA 34
SAHARA DESERT 40
GHANA 42
NIGERIA 44
NAMIBIA, BOTSWANA & ZIMBABWE 48
SOUTH AFRICA 50
PORTUGAL & SPAIN 54
UNITED KINGDOM 56
FRANCE & ITALY 58
NORWAY & SWEDEN 62

INTRODUCTION

HELLO, EXPLORER!

My name is Pastor Louie. Ever since I was your age, I have been fascinated by God's amazing world and have wanted to travel and explore it. When I was in school, I would ask my teachers if I could take home the maps from our classroom's bookshelves—and they let me! So before I'd go to sleep, I would lay them across my bedroom floor, shine a flashlight on them, and dream about all the places I could go—California, South Africa, Montana, Australia, or London. I wanted to go everywhere, and the opportunities for fun-filled adventures were endless!

I'd imagine what the people, the animals, and even the food must be like in all the unique countries I would see on the maps. What is it like to live in Ghana? What sport do people like to play in Cuba? What's it like to share a meal with friends in Japan? Hundreds of questions would swirl around in my mind as I turned the pages of the atlas.

But here is what's even more fascinating. God made the seven continents and every country and culture as unique as He made you and me. There are 195 countries in the world (and counting—countries aren't a fixed number), and each one is remarkable and one-of-a-kind, even though we couldn't feature them all. (And I encourage you to look up countries that aren't included in these pages.) Throughout this book, the Indescribable kids and I are taking you on a journey through interactive maps—learning more about things like the Angel Falls in Venezuela, the cueca dancers in Chile, the largest telescope in Czechia, and the giant anteaters in Colombia. From the top of the highest peak on Mount Everest to the lowest point in the Great Barrier Reef, we'll experience the evidence of God's handiwork all around us!

So pack your bags and get ready to go on an atlas adventure! As we encounter each destination, you'll learn new facts about incredible countries, including their awesome landforms, their amazing wild animals, and the interesting people who live there and their contributions to space. You'll even learn words from some of their languages! Most importantly, you'll see God's fingerprints on everything, and each detail you uncover will open your eyes to the wonder of God's creation.

I can't wait to start this quest together. So without further ado . . . away we go!

PASTOR LOUIE

WORLD MAP

- ARCTIC OCEAN
- ASIA
- PACIFIC OCEAN
- AFRICA
- INDIAN OCEAN
- AUSTRALIA

ARCTIC OCEAN

 Despite its big size, North America is home to **less than 10%** of the world's population.

North America is home to many major mountain ranges, including the **Rocky Mountains**, the **Appalachian Mountains**, the **Cascades**, the **Sierra Nevada**, the **Brooks Range**, the **Alaska Range**, and the **Sierra Madre** (MAW-dray).

North America is a great place to visit if you love bears, though they aren't the cuddly kind! You can find **black bears**, **brown bears**, and **polar bears** there.

FAITH
About two-thirds of North Americans are **Christians**.

ATLANTIC OCEAN

Niagara Falls is the biggest (by volume) and most famous waterfall in North America.

NORTH AMERICA

PUERTO RICO

EXPLORE THE CONTINENT **The third-largest continent, North America is made up of 23 countries** and holds more than 590 million people. It's the only continent that has all climate types, from rainforests to deserts to permanent ice caps! It's also known for its mountains, beaches, very cold regions, really warm regions, and tons of animals, like the American bison, brown bears, raccoons, and bats.

The indigenous Canadian communities (indigenous people are communities that are originally from an area), or **First Nations** peoples, have fought hard to preserve their culture through amazing art! Some of their most popular works are beautiful sculptures made from bone, woven baskets, and wood carvings.

ARCTIC OCEAN

On the Arctic Ocean you can find one of the spookiest sights in Canada called the **Smoking Hills**. This strip of red rocks is covered by towers of smoke because the rocks have been burning steadily for centuries due to a chemical reaction between the air and minerals found underground.

FAITH
Canada has no official **religion**, but more than half of Canadians are Christian.

The **Nunavut** (NEW-nuh-voot) territory is very close to the Arctic Circle. Because of this, Nunavut experiences almost a month of darkness each winter when the sun shines for only a few hours each day. If you ever visit during the winter, be sure to pack a night-light!

UNITED STATES

Mount Logan is the highest point in Canada at 19,551 feet tall. That makes it the second tallest mountain in North America after Denali in Alaska.

BEARS
Canada is home to four bear species: American brown bears (including grizzly bears), black bears, polar bears, and Kermode bears.

PACIFIC OCEAN

FAITH
In Churchill, Manitoba, polar bear sightings are so common that most people don't lock the doors to their home or car in case a bear chases them and they have to run to the nearest shelter. Hopefully you won't ever face a big polar bear in the wild, but you will face hard times in your life. **And just like the people in Churchill, you've got a place to hide when things get tough.** Nahum 1:7 says that God "gives protection in times of trouble" (ICB).

MOOSE
Moose are found almost everywhere in Canada and are even considered a Canadian symbol. A male moose can weigh up to 1,400 pounds and can run up to 35 miles per hour!

SIX-SPOTTED TIGER BEETLES
When six-spotted tiger beetles become adults, they hunt their prey (which is other kinds of insects), but when they are just young larvae, these beetles dig a hole in the ground, wait for a snack to come by, and then pounce on their dinner.

FREDERICK BANTING

LIFESPAN: November 14, 1891–February 21, 1941

BIRTHPLACE: Alliston, Ontario, Canada

Though he planned to become a pastor, Frederick studied medicine instead. He and his colleagues discovered insulin, which has helped millions of people with diabetes live longer, healthier lives. Because of this discovery, he became the youngest person to win a Nobel Prize in Medicine, receiving the award at age 32.

Ice hockey and **lacrosse** are Canada's national sports! Lacrosse was originally played by local indigenous communities in Canada, and immigrants to the country fell in love with the game too.

UNITED STATES

LEARN THE LANGUAGE

FRENCH CANADIAN SLANG

C'EST LE FUN (SEH-lah fuhn): it's awesome

METS-EN (MEH ohn): for sure

JASER (JEH-zee): to chat

WISDOM

Darkness can be scary because you can't see where you're going or what you might run into. In life, when you don't know what's ahead, **check out Psalm 119:105**, which says you have a light to guide you—God's Word.

GREENLAND

KEY FACTS

OFFICIAL LANGUAGES: French and English

CAPITAL CITY: Ottawa

NEIGHBORING COUNTRIES & BODIES OF WATER: United States, Arctic Ocean, Pacific Ocean, Atlantic Ocean

NATIONAL TREE: Maple

NATIONAL BIRD: Gray jay

NATIONAL DISH: Poutine (poo-TEEN), a French-Canadian dish of fries topped with brown gravy and cheese curds

Nearly 40% of Canada is considered **arctic** (which means extremely cold). While that part of the country isn't easy to live in, around 200,000 people live there. They are mostly indigenous (in-DIH-jih-nus) nations like the Athabascan (ath-a-BASK-in), Gwich'in (gwi-CHIN), and Inuit (IHN-yoo-uht).

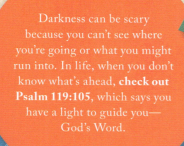

ATLANTIC PUFFINS

An Atlantic puffin can fit 61 fish inside its bill at one time. Talk about taking a big bite!

The Pingualuit (peen-gwa-LEW-it) **Crater Lake** was formed when a meteorite crashed into the surface of the Earth a long time ago. This perfectly round lake gets its water only from rainfall (so no rivers flow into the lake), and it's one of the clearest lakes in the world.

HARP SEALS

In the summers, you can find adorable harp seals in Canada. Baby harp seals, or pups, are born with fluffy white fur, but they lose this cute coat by the time they are three weeks old.

ATLANTIC OCEAN

LOVE

We're called to be mimics—but not like crows, copying voices around us! Ephesians 5:1–2 says, "**Therefore be imitators of God,** as beloved children; and walk in love, just as Christ also loved you" (NASB).

AMERICAN CROWS

You can frequently spot American crows in Canada. These smart birds can solve problems, use tools, and recognize faces. They are also talented mimics, which means they can copy sounds and voices that they hear.

Canada has a permanent spot on the **International Space Station (ISS)**, a giant research lab that orbits the Earth. Aboard the ISS, Canadian astronauts use robots to help develop technology for surgeons to use in tricky surgeries.

CANADA

OTTAWA ★

EXPLORE THE COUNTRY **Canada is at the northernmost part** of the continent of North America. Though the country takes up half of North America, its population is only 38 million people, which is roughly the same population as the US state of California. Known for its spectacular natural beauty, Canada has more lakes than every other country in the entire world combined! Even sweeter, Canada produces 75% of the world's maple syrup, thanks to its wealth of maple trees.

UNITED STATES

EXPLORE THE COUNTRY

The United States of America (USA or US) is situated between **Canada and Mexico** and has over 330 million people living in it. It has the third-largest population of any country in the world! Known as "the melting pot," the US has many cultures and races represented in one nation. The terrain varies across the land: to the west you'll find deserts, in the southeast you'll find tropical beaches, and to the north you can find chilly mountain peaks. This also means the animal life is diverse, with American bison, brown bears, and even bald eagles found in the country.

WESTERN SKINK LIZARDS
The Western skink lizard can escape predators by using something called autotomy, which means it can detach its own tail in self-defense. The detached tail will keep moving around, distracting predators so the skink can escape!

The longest river in the US is the **Missouri River**, measuring at an amazing 2,341 miles long. The river begins in the Rocky Mountains in Montana and ends near St. Louis, where it joins the Mississippi River.

AMERICAN BISON
The American bison is the national mammal of the US. It is the largest mammal in North America, and a male bison (or bull) can weigh around 2,000 pounds.

ROCKY MOUNTAINS

SIERRA NEVADA

PINK RATTLESNAKES
Don't let the cute color fool you! The pink rattlesnake is just as venomous as any other rattlesnake, but its color helps it blend in with the rocks of the Grand Canyon, so it's harder to spot.

The US is home to the **Grand Canyon**, a massive canyon (a super-deep valley) found in the state of Arizona. The canyon is 1,904 square miles—bigger than the entire state of Rhode Island!

ALASKA
The US goverment recognizes **574 different indigenous people groups**. About 40% of these groups are found in Alaska.

Redwood National and State Parks in California are home to redwood forests that house the tallest tree on Earth, known as Hyperion. Hyperion is 380 feet tall. You'd have to stack almost 38 basketball goals on top of one another to reach that height!

MEXICO

CANADA

You can't drive to **Juneau, Alaska**. Alaska's state capital is only accessible by plane or boat!

PACIFIC OCEAN

BILLY GRAHAM
LIFESPAN: November 7, 1918– February 21, 2018
BIRTHPLACE: Charlotte, North Carolina

Billy was an evangelist (a person who tells others about Jesus) who traveled the world with the message that anyone who believed in Jesus could be saved. His simple but powerful message helped lead many people to Christ.

LEARN THE LANGUAGE

AMERICAN IDIOMS

An idiom is a word or phrase that means something different from what it literally says.

YOU HAVE ANTS IN YOUR PANTS: This means you can't sit still.

I'M ALL EARS: This lets someone know you are ready to listen.

IT COSTS AN ARM AND A LEG: This means something is expensive.

IT'S A PIECE OF CAKE: This describes something easy to do.

BALD EAGLES

You might assume the bald eagle has an intimidating call (or sound), but these birds actually have an unimpressive high-pitched chirp or whistle. In fact, most movies that feature the sound of a bald-eagle cry use recordings of a red-tailed hawk.

CANADA

The biggest lake in the US is **Lake Superior**, covering 31,700 square miles.

Though there is no official religion, about 64% of US citizens are Christian.

WASHINGTON, DC

The Statue of Liberty and the Empire State Building are two of the top tourist attractions in New York City.

SpaceX is a modern space-exploration company that is working to build a thriving, livable city on the planet Mars by around 2040.

APPALACHIAN MOUNTAINS

The three major mountain ranges found in the United States are the **Rocky Mountains** (also called the Rockies), the **Appalachian Mountains**, and the **Sierra Nevada**.

In 1969, the US space program, NASA (National Aeronautics and Space Administration), sent the **Apollo 11** spacecraft to the moon, the first-ever manned moon-landing mission. American astronaut Neil Armstrong was the first man ever to walk on the moon.

Key Facts

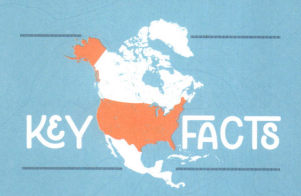

OFFICIAL LANGUAGE: Though there is no official language, English is most commonly spoken

CAPITAL CITY: Washington, DC

NEIGHBORING COUNTRIES & BODIES OF WATER: Canada, Mexico, Atlantic Ocean, Pacific Ocean, Gulf of Mexico

NATIONAL TREE: Oak

NATIONAL BIRD: Bald eagle

NATIONAL DISH: Though there is no official national dish, the US is known for hamburgers and apple pie

MANATEES

At the Chassahowitzka (CHASS-uh-how-ITZ-kuh) National Wildlife Refuge in Florida, you can spot manatees along the Gulf Coast during the winter. Even though manatees are huge creatures sometimes called sea cows, they are believed to be the source of a lot of old mermaid folktales.

GULF OF MEXICO

ATLANTIC OCEAN

CUBA

HAITI

DOMINICAN REPUBLIC

PUERTO RICO

HAWAII

There are 169 active volcanoes in the US! In fact, one of the most active volcanoes on Earth, **Kilauea** (kee-la-WAY-uh), is found in Hawaii.

CHRIST'S LOVE

Ephesians 3:18 says, "**I pray that you and all God's holy people will have the power to understand the greatness of Christ's love.** I pray that you can understand how wide and how long and how high and how deep that love is" (ICB). Whenever you need to remember how wide, long, high, and deep God's love for you is, just picture how great the Grand Canyon is!

DR. MARTIN LUTHER KING JR.

LIFESPAN: January 15, 1929–April 4, 1968
BIRTHPLACE: Atlanta, Georgia

Dr. King was a pastor and key leader in the civil rights movement in the US. The movement fought for equality for all Americans by targeting unjust laws that oppressed Black citizens. Dr. King's faith in God gave him courage to fight against unfair laws and to do the right thing.

Because of the many cultures found in the US, the music is incredibly diverse, with genres like jazz, hip-hop, country, bluegrass, R&B, gospel, and rock and roll.

AMAZING

CARIBBEAN SEA

UNITED STATES

The lowest point in Mexico is the **Laguna Salada** (meaning "salty lagoon"), which sits 33 feet below sea level. This lake is in the middle of a desert, so when it completely dries up, dust storms can occur.

In Sonora, Mexico, you can see the **boojum tree**, which looks like an upside-down carrot. The tree is covered in spines that produce yellow flowers that grow in bunches. It also has a hollow trunk where bees love to build nests.

In Mexico, when a girl turns 15, she marks the occasion with a quinceañera (KEENT-say-uh-NYAR-uh), which celebrates that a girl is growing up. Traditionally, the birthday girl would attend a church service, called mass, followed by a party, in which she would wear a beautiful dress and enjoy food, music, and dancing.

FLYING SQUIRRELS

Flying squirrels don't actually fly, but they can spread out their folds of skin to glide from tree to tree. The longest recorded glide was about 295 feet. That's about the same length as the Statue of Liberty's height!

Mexico is part of the **Ring of Fire**, which is a horseshoe-shaped area of the Pacific Ocean where volcanoes and earthquakes are common. A whopping 75% of active volcanoes and 90% of earthquakes occur along the Ring of Fire!

MONARCH BUTTERFLIES

Endangered monarch butterflies migrate every year from Canada and the US to central Mexico, where they spend the winter.

Mexico does not have an official religion, but more than 80% of Mexicans are Roman Catholic.

Hidden Beach is a unique beach in a big cavern into which waters from the Pacific Ocean flow. The only way to reach Hidden Beach is by swimming or kayaking down a long water tunnel.

AMAZING!

Did you know Mexico City was built on a lake, and the city sinks a little each year? That shows how important it is to build important things on a solid foundation. In Matthew 7:24–27, **Jesus reminded us that we also need to build our lives on a solid foundation**, which is another way of saying we should place our trust, hope, and future plans in Him.

The highest point in Mexico is **Pico de Orizaba** (PEE-co day or-ee-ZAH-bah), an inactive volcano that reaches 18,406 feet above sea level.

PACIFIC OCEAN

Popocatépetl (po-po-ca-TEH-pet-uhl), an active volcano, is the second-highest point in the country at 17,749 feet above sea level.

★ MEXICO CITY

LEARN THE LANGUAGE

SPANISH

BUENOS DÍAS (bwe-NOS DEE-ahs): good morning

BUENOS TARDES (bwe-NOS TAR-deyz): good afternoon

BUENOS NOCHES (bwe-NOS NO-cheyz): good evening

MIGUEL HIDALGO Y COSTILLA

LIFESPAN: May 8, 1753–July 30, 1811
BIRTHPLACE: Guanajuato, Mexico

Miguel was a Catholic priest who worked hard for political change. His fight for Mexico's freedom from Spanish rule was so influential that he is known as the "father of Mexican independence."

AXOLOTLS

One of the only places in the world where you can find the axolotl (ax-oh-LAWT-ul) is in Lake Xochimilco (SO-chee-MEEL-co) in Mexico City! These members of the salamander family may look like lizards, but they have gills, so they live underwater.

14

MEXICO

KEY FACTS

OFFICIAL LANGUAGE: Spanish

CAPITAL CITY: Mexico City

NEIGHBORING COUNTRIES & BODIES OF WATER: United States, Guatemala, Belize, Atlantic Ocean, Gulf of Mexico, Pacific Ocean

NATIONAL TREE: Montezuma baldcypress

NATIONAL BIRD: Golden eagle

NATIONAL DISH: Mole (MOE-lay), a sauce that may contain nuts, fruits, chiles, and even chocolate

EXPLORE THE COUNTRY Located south of the United States, Mexico has a population of approximately 129 million people. About 60% of the population is Mestizo, people with a mix of Native American and Spanish blood. Mexico's land has high mountains, deep valleys, dry deserts, and dense rainforests. You can find beautiful plants across the country, from short grasses and bright-green ferns to prickly cacti and unique trees, including the boojum tree. It's also home to a wide range of animals, from monkeys and anteaters to rabbits and armadillos!

A legend says the **Yucatán Peninsula** in Mexico got its name after a Spanish explorer had a confusing conversation with a Mayan local. The explorer asked the name of the peninsula, and the Mayan said, "Ma'anaatik ka t'ann," which means, "I don't understand you." The explorer misunderstood and thought the Mayan had replied, "Yucatán."

WHOA

EMILIANO ZAPATA

LIFESPAN: August 8, 1879– April 10, 1919

BIRTHPLACE: Anenecuilco, Mexico

Emiliano fought for Mexican independence during the Mexican Revolution from 1910–1920. A strong Catholic, he used his faith as motivation to fight for freedom for his people. To this day, he is one of the most revered revolutionaries (someone who fights for political change) in Mexican history.

Underneath the Yucatán Peninsula is the **Chicxulub** (CHICK-sooh-loob) crater, one of the largest craters found on Earth, measuring over 110 miles wide. To create such a large crater, the asteroid or comet that hit the Earth must have been over eight miles in diameter.

Did you know you can visit pyramids in Mexico? In **Tulum** and **Chichén Itzá** (CHI-chin EET-za) you can see pyramids from ancient **Mayan** and **Teotihuacán** (tee-oh-tee-WA-cahn) civilizations.

GULF OF MEXICO

WHALE SHARKS
Whale sharks can grow up to 59 feet long and weigh around 15 tons (twice as heavy as the average elephant). But don't let their gigantic size scare you! They are filter feeders (meaning they eat tiny organisms found in seawater), so they're harmless to humans.

BELIZE

GUATEMALA

HONDURAS

NICARAGUA

AWESOME

One of the most iconic forms of folk music from Mexico is called mariachi (mah-ree-AAH-chee). **A mariachi band is made of a group of singers and musicians playing guitars, violins, the bass, trumpets, and a five-string guitar called a vihuela** (vuh-WAY-luh). The musicians usually wear suits and sombreros (hats) decorated with silver or gold.

CACOMISTLES
The cacomistle is a mammal in the raccoon family. It weighs only a couple of pounds but can grow up to about 40 inches long, though most of that length comes from its tail. Like raccoons, the cacomistle is nocturnal (meaning active at night) and eats mostly fruits, veggies, and some smaller animals.

KEY FACTS

OFFICIAL LANGUAGE: Spanish

CAPITAL CITY: San José

NEIGHBORING COUNTRIES & BODIES OF WATER: Nicaragua, Panama, Caribbean Sea, Pacific Ocean

NATIONAL TREE: Guanacaste

NATIONAL BIRD: Clay-colored thrush, known as the yigüirro

NATIONAL DISH: Gallo pinto (ga-YO peen-toh), a dish served mainly for breakfast made of black beans and fried rice

Costa Rica got rid of its military in 1948 and created an **"army of teachers"** instead. And that army has done good work! Costa Rica has one of the highest **literacy** (which means people can read and write) rates in Latin America! (Latin America includes Mexico, Central America, South America, and some neighboring islands.)

The **Arenal Volcano** was the most active volcano in Costa Rica from 1968 until 2010, but it's now in a "resting" phase. This means it isn't at risk of erupting in the near future.

Rio Celeste, which means "light blue river," runs through the Tenorio Volcano National Park. The nearby volcanic activity produces lots of sulfur and carbonate, which turns the river's waters a stunning turquoise color.

SLOTHS

Costa Rica is home to two species of sloth: the brown-throated three-toed sloth and the Hoffman's two-toed sloth. You'll usually find sloths hanging upside down from tree branches, but you might spot them swimming in a river!

BE STILL

Sloths are known for their slow movements, and sometimes we need to slow down too. Psalm 46:10 says, **"Be still and know that I am God"** (ICB). So whether you're busy with schoolwork or sports or something else, take some time to talk to God. Thank Him for every good thing He has given you.

JORGE VOLIO JIMÉNEZ

LIFESPAN: August 26, 1882–October 20, 1955
BIRTHPLACE: Cartago, Costa Rica

Jorge became a priest in 1909, using his faith and education to fight for justice. Later he became a journalist and professor and worked hard for the fair treatment of the poor and for equality among Costa Rican citizens.

In 2021, Costa Rica announced that it would be developing its own **space program**, focusing on peaceful space-exploration missions, new technology, and research to find ways to use Earth's resources responsibly.

PACIFIC OCEAN

COSTA RICA

EXPLORE THE COUNTRY **Costa Rica is in the southern tip of North America.** It has a population of more than 5 million and has the highest percentage of people of Spanish descent of any Central American country. (Central America is the southern region of North America, between Mexico and South America.) Costa Rica's beautiful coastal plains are separated by mountains and several active volcanoes. And it's home to incredible wildlife, from sloths and toucans to weasels and iguanas.

NICARAGUA

TOUCANS
Six species of toucan are found in Costa Rica, but the largest is the black-mandibled toucan, also known as the yellow-throated toucan, which can grow up to two feet tall.

The "**air plants**" in Costa Rica don't have any roots to keep them in the ground. Instead, they root themselves to a nearby plant or tree and get nutrients from the rain and air.

Costa Rica has large **banana plantations** on the Caribbean coast. In fact, one out of every 10 bananas eaten across the world comes from Costa Rica!

CARIBBEAN SEA

SOR MARIA ROMERO MENESES

LIFESPAN: January 13, 1902–July 7, 1977
BIRTHPLACE: Granada, Nicaragua

Maria was a beloved nun. Arriving in Costa Rica in 1931, she worked to help feed the hungry and find homes for the homeless. She was also a strong supporter of education, starting schools and providing homes and training for girls in need.

GET ROOTED

Air plants stay alive by rooting themselves to living things around them. As Christians, we get the opportunity to root ourselves to God! **Jeremiah 17:7–8** says, "Blessed is the one who trusts in the LORD, whose confidence is in him. They will be like a tree planted by the water that sends out its roots by the stream" (NIV).

★ **SAN JOSÉ**

Mount Chirripó (chee-REE-poh) is the highest point in Costa Rica, reaching an impressive 12,532 feet high. You'd have to stack the Great Pyramid of Giza in Egypt on top of itself over 27 times to reach that height!

PANAMA

POISONOUS DART FROGS
Poisonous dart frogs are incredibly colorful and emit a deadly toxin from their skin. The strawberry poison dart frog is mostly red with dark blueish-purple legs, so it's sometimes known as the blue jeans frog.

FAITH
Though Costa Rica has no national religion, **about 85% are Christians.**

LEARN THE LANGUAGE

SPANISH

Spanish is the primary language of Costa Rica, but a unique part of Costa Rican Spanish is the use of "tico" or "tica" at the end of some words, which means something is cute or tiny.

PERRITICO (PARE-uh-TEE-coh): little dog

GATICO (gah-TEE-coh): little cat

AMIGITO (AH-mih-GEE-toh): little friend

CAIMANS
Caimans are cousins to crocodiles, but they're much smaller, only reaching about six feet in length. You'll find these creatures relaxing on the shores of rivers and swamps.

Costa Ricans are serious about protecting the Earth and have set aside over 25% of the land as **wildlife preserves** and **national parks**. That percentage of protected land is larger than any other country's in the world!

CUBA

The first Cuban to fly into space was **Arnaldo Tamayo Méndez**, an astronaut with the Soviet Union who traveled to space in the Soyuz 38 on September 18, 1980. The mission lasted eight days, and when Méndez returned, Fidel Castro (the former leader of Cuba) awarded him with the title of Hero of the Republic of Cuba.

EXPLORE THE COUNTRY The largest island in the Caribbean Sea, Cuba is about 42,000 square miles (or about the size of the US state of Tennessee). Across the country, you'll find beautiful mountain forests, thick jungles, and soft grasslands. About 11 million people live there, along with some amazing animals, like the Cuban hutia, the bee hummingbird, the French angelfish, and the Cuban crocodile.

Royal palm trees can grow to 75 feet tall and are found all over the country.

GULF OF MEXICO

★ HAVANA

BEE HUMMINGBIRDS
Cuba is home to the bee hummingbird. While hummingbirds are already small, this particular species is the smallest bird in the entire world. It's so tiny that it weighs less than a penny!

Cuba is the perfect place for insect lovers to visit. The country is home to **over 7,000 species of insects** as well as arachnids like tarantulas and scorpions.

Topes de Collantes (co-YAHN-tays) is a huge nature reserve that protects wildlife. It's full of lush jungle, amazing waterfalls, and lots of caves and natural swimming holes.

The oldest city in Cuba is **Baracoa**, founded in 1512.

FRENCH ANGELFISH
Thanks to their thin bodies, French angelfish can swim through narrow spaces, which helps them hide from predators.

LEARN THE LANGUAGE

SPANISH

HOLA (oh-LA): hello

ADIÓS (AH-dee-os): goodbye

ME LLAMO (may YA-mo): my name is

GRACIAS (GRAH-see-uhs): thank you

REVEREND ERELIO MARTINEZ GARCIA

LIFESPAN: c. 1926–2005
BIRTHPLACE: Cuba

Erelio was a Cuban pastor and evangelist. Even though being a Christian and spreading the gospel was dangerous during his lifetime, he constantly did what he could to spread the Word of God to his fellow Cubans.

ATLANTIC OCEAN

📍 THE BAHAMAS

Cuba has been involved in many wars and fights for independence. But the Bible says that in heaven, fights for freedom and justice won't need to happen. **In heaven, everything will be perfect, and everyone's needs will be met.** In fact, Revelation 7:15–17 says there will be no more tears, and no one will be hungry or thirsty.

SOME DAY!

KEY FACTS

OFFICIAL LANGUAGE: Spanish

CAPITAL CITY: Havana

NEIGHBORING BODIES OF WATER: Gulf of Mexico, Caribbean Sea, Atlantic Ocean

NATIONAL TREE: Royal palm

NATIONAL BIRD: Cuban trogon (also called tocororo)

NATIONAL DISH: Ropa vieja (RO-pah VEE-eh-ha), which means "old clothes," is beef served in a tomato sauce with veggies that is slow cooked until the meat is tender

BUTTERFLY BATS
The butterfly bat, one of the smallest species of bat in the world, has a wingspan of about five inches long and often weighs less than an ounce (lighter than a pencil!).

FAITH
Cuba does not have an official religion, but **about 60%** are Christian.

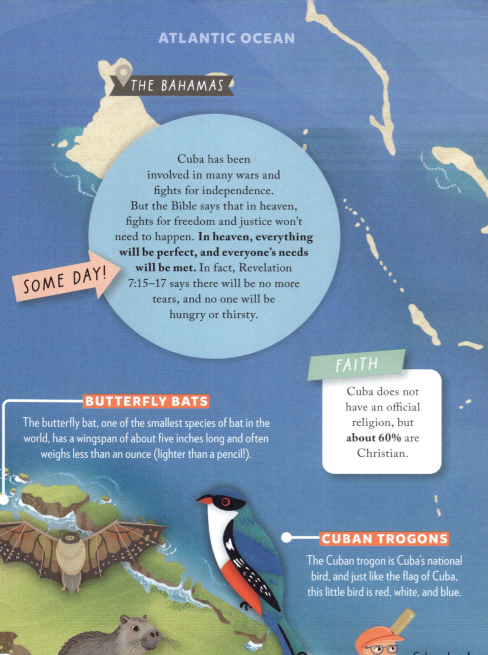

CUBAN TROGONS
The Cuban trogon is Cuba's national bird, and just like the flag of Cuba, this little bird is red, white, and blue.

CUBAN HUTIAS
The Cuban hutia is a furry rodent with a long tail that lives among the trees. According to legend, the hutia was the first meat that Christopher Columbus ate in the New World.

Cubans love **baseball**! In fact, the country has 16 professional teams.

CUBAN BOA SNAKES
The Cuban boa snake can grow to 21 feet long (an average adult human male is almost 6 feet tall). These snakes aren't venomous, but they hunt in groups and form what is called a "curtain of snakes" at cave entrances to catch their favorite snack: bats!

Cuba's highest point is found in the Sierra Maestra mountain range. **Turquino Peak** reaches a whopping 6,476 feet above sea level.

No place on the island of Cuba goes below sea level, so the lowest point is the beginning of the **Caribbean Sea** and **Atlantic Ocean**.

Cuban music styles like **rumba, bolero, conga, salsa,** and **son Cubano** have Spanish and African roots. These unique sounds will have you dancing in no time!

AMAZING!
The bee hummingbird may be small, but God takes care of even the tiniest creatures. And He cares even more for you! Matthew 6:26 says, "Look at the birds in the air. They don't plant or harvest or store food in barns. But your heavenly Father feeds the birds. And you know that you are worth much more than the birds" (ICB).

📍 JAMAICA

📍 HAITI

CARIBBEAN SEA

PACIFIC OCEAN

The **Galápagos giant tortoise** is the largest tortoise in the world, weighing around 500 pounds. On average, it lives more than a hundred years and can go a year without food or water.

The **green anaconda** loves to hunt in the water, keeping most of its body underwater with just the top of its head over the surface of the water. It can eat large prey, from wild pigs to capybaras to jaguars!

The **Andes Mountains** is the longest continental mountain range in the world. It covers over 4,000 miles and sits across a whopping seven countries: Venezuela, Colombia, Peru, Bolivia, Ecuador, Argentina, and Chile.

Capybaras, the largest rodent in the world, are known for being friendly. In fact, you might find them snuggling with ducks, puppies, goats, and even monkeys!

SOUTH AMERICA

EXPLORE THE CONTINENT **South America is the fourth-largest continent in the entire world.** The name *America* comes from the name of the Italian explorer Amerigo Vespucci (vuh-SPOO-chee). Vespucci was one of the earliest explorers to the continent. At first, the term *America* referred only to what we know as South America today, but now the "Americas" refer to South America and North America. Made up of 12 countries with over 440 million people, South America has diverse geography, with rainforests (like the famous Amazon Rainforest), deserts, and mountains. It also has an incredible range of wildlife, from piranhas to monkeys to toucans!

AMAZING!

Maybe a mud bath really does have health benefits! One time, Jesus used mud and a bath to heal a man who had been born blind. "[Jesus] spit on the ground and made some mud with it. He put the mud on the man's eyes. Then he told the man, 'Go and wash in the Pool of Siloam.' (Siloam means Sent.) So the man went to the pool. **He washed and came back. And he was able to see**" (John 9:6-7 ICB).

SAINT LAURA MONTOYA UPEGUI

LIFESPAN: May 26, 1874–October 21, 1949
BIRTHPLACE: Jericó, Colombia

When Laura was young, her mother taught her to love all people. Many years later, Laura became a missionary. And even though others told her she was wasting her time, Laura traveled to indigenous people groups of South America and shared the gospel with them.

KEY FACTS

OFFICIAL LANGUAGE: Spanish

CAPITAL CITY: Bogotá

NEIGHBORING COUNTRIES & BODIES OF WATER: Ecuador, the Pacific Ocean, Panama, the Caribbean Sea, Venezuela, Brazil, Peru

NATIONAL TREE: Wax palm

NATIONAL BIRD: Andean condor

NATIONAL DISH: Bandeja paisa (band-AY-ha PIE-za), a warm and filling dish of tasty things like red beans, white rice, fried pork rinds called chich arron, spicy sausage called chorizo, a fried egg, a cake made of ground corn called arepa, plantains, and avocado

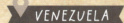 VENEZUELA

89'98 BUTTERFLIES

Of the 3,642 species of butterflies in Colombia, the coolest has got to be the 89'98 butterfly. It gets its name because of the patterns on its wings that look like the numbers 89 and 98 written in bubble numbers!

Colombians love to dance, and each year they hold the world's largest salsa (dancing, not the kind served with tortilla chips!) festival. The **World Salsa Festival** can bring in crowds of over 40,000 people!

 GUYANA

BRAZIL

HALLELUJAH!

Colombia is known for its love of music and dance, which can be used to express big feelings, tell stories, or even teach lessons. **Christians can also use music and dance to worship and praise God.** Psalm 149:3 says, "They should praise him with dancing. They should praise him with tambourines and harps" (ICB).

COLOMBIA

EXPLORE THE COUNTRY

In the northern region of South America sits Colombia, a country with more than 50 million people with about 85 different ethnic groups. The equator crosses the bottom of Colombia, giving the country a tropical climate with a variety of soils and plants, from lush mosses to beautiful orchids to the giant American bamboo. Animals like Andean bears, sloths, and pumas love to call this country home.

KEY FACTS

OFFICIAL LANGUAGE: Spanish

CAPITAL CITY: Caracas

NEIGHBORING COUNTRIES & BODIES OF WATER: Colombia, Caribbean Sea, Atlantic Ocean, Guyana, Brazil

NATIONAL TREE: Araguaney

NATIONAL BIRD: Venezuelan troupial

NATIONAL DISH: Pabellon criollo (pa-bey-YON cri-OH-yo), a dish made of shredded beef, black beans, and rice served with fried eggs or fried plantains

The Venezuelan government helps fund organizations that protect the arts, like the popular **Simón Bolívar Symphony Orchestra**. The orchestra helps preserve Venezuelan culture and reflects the people's love for their country.

BROWN SPIDER MONKEYS
Brown spider monkeys hug when they meet each other, even intertwining their tails.

LAKE MARACAIBO

ANDES MOUNTAINS

At over 153 feet high, the **Virgin Mary of Trujillo** (true-HEE-yo) is one of the tallest statues in the world and one of the most visited attractions in Venezuela.

PACIFIC OCEAN

Joropo (hoh-ROH-poh), which means "party," has become one of the most beloved music and dance styles in Venezuela. In fact, it is the country's national dance.

SUSANA PAZ CASTILLO RAMIREZ

LIFESPAN: August 11, 1863– January 31, 1940

BIRTHPLACE: Altagracia de Orituco, Guarico, Venezuela

Susana joined a small group of women to run Saint Anthony's Hospital, where she devoted her life to helping the sick. Their motto was "God is love." Susana was known for her humility and love of prayer.

COLOMBIA

DID YOU KNOW?

The basilisk lizard isn't the only one who has stepped across the surface of the water. Jesus also walked on water! You can find this Bible story in Matthew 14:22–36, Mark 6:45–56, and John 6:16–21. But when Jesus walked on water, it wasn't because of a special foot design. It's because **He is the Son of God, which means He is fully man and fully God, and He can do anything!**

VENEZUELA

EXPLORE THE COUNTRY **Located at the north end of South America,** Venezuela is home to more than 33 million people and more than 40 languages. It has a beautiful landscape of mountains, jungles, forests, coastal plains, lakes, and even some amazing waterfalls. About half of the land is forests, but savanna grasses, swamps, and tree ferns also spread across the country. And because it has so many types of terrain and plants, you'll find a wide variety of animals too—including ocelots, spider monkeys, bears, piranhas, lizards, and much more! In fact, it holds so many types of animals that it's considered one of 17 megadiverse countries in the whole world. (That means it has more different species of animals than other countries!)

Los Roques is one of Venezuela's archipelagos (arc-ih-PEL-uh-gohz), or group of islands. It has over 300 individual islands!

At 9,072 feet, **Pico Naiguatá** is the highest peak of the Venezuelan coastal mountain range.

CHECK IT OUT

Creation reminds us how creative, strong, loving, and powerful God is. Psalm 95:4–6 says, "The deepest places on earth are his. And the highest mountains belong to him. The sea is his because he made it. He created the land with his own hands. Come, let's bow down and worship him. Let's kneel before the Lord who made us" (ICB).

ATLANTIC OCEAN

CARACAS

When you visit the **Humboldt Planetarium** in Caracas, you can check out the Zeiss projector, which lets visitors to the planetarium feel like they are in the middle of space exploring the stars!

AMAZONIAN ROYAL FLYCATCHERS

When Amazonian royal flycatchers are looking for a mate, these birds flash a bunch of colorful feathers on their head (like a fancy hat!) to attract other flycatchers.

OCELOTS

Ocelots are often found in tropical forests and like to sleep on the low branches of trees. At night, they hunt small prey like deer, monkeys, fish, and even amphibians!

The world's highest waterfall is **Angel Falls**. Its waters splash down from over 3,000 feet high!

JAGUARS

Jaguars, found mostly in the jungles of the Amazon, are not only expert hunters, but they are also the biggest feline in the Americas!

BASILISK LIZARDS

The basilisk lizard can run on the surface of the water, thanks to the unique design of their feet. And they really move! These lizards can run up to 15 miles per hour.

GUYANA

Venezuela has many tall, pointy mountains, but it also has mountains that are flat on the top, like a big table. These are called **tepuis** (tay-PWEES).

PIRANHAS

The piranha has scary-sharp teeth that act like scissors and rip through meat quickly. These fish don't typically attack humans, but swimmers need to be especially careful when water levels are low and food is scarce.

BRAZIL

FUN FACT! Venezuela has a traditional form of bullfighting called **toros coleados** (TOR-ohs col-ee-AH-dos), in which a bullfighter tries to catch and bring down a bull by its tail.

JUAN DE FRÍAS

LIFESPAN: Birth unknown–May 30, 1688
BIRTHPLACE: Caracas, Venezuela

Juan de Frías was a Lutheran priest who was arrested in 1672 for his faith in Jesus. He was kept in prison for 16 years and then sentenced to death because of his faith. But he never stopped proclaiming his love for Jesus.

LEARN THE LANGUAGE

INFORMAL VENEZUELAN SPANISH

CHAMO (CHAM-oh): dude; bro

PANA (PAN-uh): friend; friendly

BURDA (BOOR-dah): a lot

COROTO (koh-ROH-toh): belongings (like the words *stuff* or *things*)

FAITH

Around 90% of Peruvians identify as Christians. About 76% are Catholic, and 14% are Protestant. A small percentage are Jewish, Muslim, or Buddhist, or identify with another religious group. And still others have no religious views at all.

SAINT ROSE OF LIMA

LIFESPAN: April 20, 1586–August 24, 1617

BIRTHPLACE: Lima, Peru

Rose was born into a noble family. Her parents didn't want her to become a nun, but she was finally allowed to at the age of 20. Though she died at the age of 31, she spent her entire life praying, fasting, and trying to be closer to God. Her faith was so inspiring, the Catholic Church officially named her as a saint in 1671.

KEY FACTS

OFFICIAL LANGUAGE: Spanish

CAPITAL CITY: Lima

NEIGHBORING COUNTRIES & BODIES OF WATER: Pacific Ocean, Ecuador, Colombia, Brazil, Bolivia, Chile

NATIONAL TREE: Cinchona (sin-KOH-nuh)

NATIONAL BIRD: Andean cock-of-the-rock

NATIONAL DISH: Ceviche, a dish made of fresh raw fish marinated in lime along with salt, garlic, peppers, and onions

PERUVIAN HAIRLESS DOGS

The Peruvian hairless dog, the only dog breed native to Peru, has its own holiday on June 12: Day of the Peruvian Hairless Dog!

Weaving is an important art for Peruvians, who are famous for their traditional ponchos. But these ponchos aren't simple to make! It takes a weaver up to 600 hours to complete one of these ponchos.

BRAZIL

Peru is one of the leading fishing countries in the world. They catch and sell mackerel, tuna, swordfish, anchoveta (which is part of the anchovy family), and much more!

FOLLOW ME

Fishing was an important industry in Bible times. In fact, several of Jesus' disciples were fishermen. But when Jesus met them, He said, **"Come follow me. I will make you fishermen for men"** (Matthew 4:19 ICB). After following Jesus, the disciples no longer caught fish. They "caught" people by telling them about Jesus and the way to heaven.

Machu Picchu is the name of the ancient ruins site built by the Incan civilization around 1450. It spans more than five miles, and it has more than 150 buildings and 3,000 steps carved from stone. It's the most popular attraction in Peru today!

BOLIVIA

SAINT MARTIN DE PORRES

LIFESPAN: December 9, 1579–November 3, 1639

BIRTHPLACE: Lima, Peru

Martin took care of the helpless and sick. He helped start a children's hospital and an orphanage, and he even took care of sick animals. He helped nurse injured or sick cats, dogs, mice, and rats back to health.

LAKE TITICACA

PERU

EXPLORE THE COUNTRY

On the western coast of South America, Peru is a tropical country that is just south of the equator. Its land is made up of three main regions: the Amazonia (the areas near the Amazon River), the Andes Mountains, and the coastal plains. Because of its coastal waters, Peru is home to a ton of fish and bird species, including tuna, swordfish, pelicans, and Humboldt penguins. More than 33 million residents enjoy Peru's natural beauty.

KEY FACTS

OFFICIAL LANGUAGE: Portuguese

CAPITAL CITY: Brasília

NEIGHBORING COUNTRIES & BODIES OF WATER: Brazil shares a border with every country in South America but Chile and Ecuador, and its east coast sits against the Atlantic Ocean

NATIONAL TREE: Pau brasil

NATIONAL BIRD: Rufous-bellied thrush

NATIONAL DISH: Feijoada (fey-JWAH-duh), a stew made of black beans and different kinds of salted and smoked pork and beef

COLOMBIA

VENEZUELA

The highest mountain in Brazil is **Pico da Neblina**. It's over 9,000 feet tall, which is as high as stacking more than nine Eiffel Towers on top of one another!

ECUADOR

JAGUARS

Jaguars, Brazil's national animal, are the third-largest big cat in the world behind lions and tigers, but their bite is the strongest among all types of big cats.

PELÉ

LIFESPAN: October 23, 1940–December 29, 2022
BIRTHPLACE: Três Corações, Brazil

Edson Arantes do Nascimento, also known as Pelé, is considered to be one of the best football players ever. He helped the Brazilian national football team win three World Cups in 1958, 1962, and 1970, and he often praised God for his athletic abilities.

Football (or soccer in the US) is the most popular sport in Brazil, and Brazilians are great at it! Brazil has won the FIFA World Cup (a tournament to determine the world champion) five times.

BOLIVIA

PERU

PACIFIC OCEAN

BRAZIL

EXPLORE THE COUNTRY

Taking up about half of the continent (more than 3 million square miles), Brazil is the largest country in South America. It even spans four different time zones! More than 216 million people live there. In fact, it has over 300 different ethnic groups as well as many indigenous people groups that are isolated, which means they don't have contact with other people groups or the modern world. Filled with wetlands, rivers, mountains, and plateaus, Brazil has a beautiful landscape that makes a perfect home for animals like jaguars, monkeys, roadrunners, a variety of birds, and much more.

LEARN THE LANGUAGE

INFORMAL PORTUGUESE

OLÁ (OH-lah): hello

COMO VOCÊ ESTÁ (CO-moh voh-say es-tah): How are you?

BOM DIA (BOHM dee-ah): good morning

BOA TARDE (BO-uh TAR-day): good afternoon

ADEUS (AH-de-yus): goodbye

AMAZON RAINFOREST

You can see the Amazon Rainforest from **space**! Images taken from satellites orbiting Earth can help scientists monitor the health of the rainforest.

You can hear the cry of a **red howler monkey** from three miles away!

SHELTER

When you have bad days, you may need some shelter from your troubles—but you won't find it in the kapok tree! Go to God to find comfort and shelter. **Psalm 27:5** says, "During danger he will keep me safe in his shelter. He will hide me in his Holy Tent" (ICB).

The **giant monkey frog** has a waxy layer on its skin to protect it from the sun.

The **giant water lily** can grow up to 10 feet in diameter and can hold up to 60 pounds of weight.

EXPLORE THE ECOSYSTEM

The Amazon Rainforest covers over 2 million miles of South America and is the most diverse place on Earth for plant and animal life, with 427 species of mammals, 1,300 different types of birds, 378 reptile species, and over 400 amphibians. It's also home to about 30 million people.

Kapok trees are super tall and provide shelter for frogs and snakes in their trunks.

Deforestation (the destruction of forests) has massively damaged the Amazon Rainforest. Thankfully, as people are becoming more aware of the harm that comes from destroying a natural habitat, conservation efforts have helped slow down forest loss.

The Amazon Rainforest is home to 15% of the world's **birds** and **butterflies!**

Candy bars don't grow on trees, but cocoa beans do! The seeds of the **cacao** (cuh-COW) trees are used to make chocolate.

The largest animal in the Amazon basin is the **black caiman**, which is also the largest species of alligator. These creatures can grow to 20 feet in length and live up to 80 years! Their black scales make them great night hunters and help them absorb heat during the day.

It's important to discover new things that God filled the Earth with. Even though these discoveries are new to us, they're not new to God. In fact, God knows every hair on your head (Luke 12:7) and every animal and plant in the world! Just like scientists are discovering new species in the Amazon, you can discover more about God by reading His Word, spending time in prayer, and remembering that every amazing animal and plant you find on Earth is a gift from God!

New species of creatures are constantly being discovered in the Amazon Rainforest. In the last decade, scientists have identified **10,000 new species of beetles** alone!

The **coffee plant** sprouts red fruits that contain seeds, called coffee beans, which are used to brew—you guessed it—coffee! And because of those beans, the coffee plant is the most-consumed plant in the entire world.

KEY FACTS

OFFICIAL LANGUAGE: Spanish

CAPITAL CITY: Santiago

NEIGHBORING COUNTRIES & BODIES OF WATER: Pacific Ocean, Peru, Bolivia, Argentina

NATIONAL TREE: Chilean pine (or monkey puzzle tree)

NATIONAL BIRD: Andean condor

NATIONAL DISH: Empanadas, a baked pastry filled with different types of meat and veggies

PACIFIC OCEAN

ALBERTO HURTADO CRUCHAGA

LIFESPAN: January 22, 1901– August 18, 1952

BIRTHPLACE: Viña del Mar, Chile

When Alberto became a priest, he encouraged his community to help the poor, taught them about Christ, gave them places to live, and helped them learn a trade so they could support themselves and their families.

VICUÑAS

The wool of a vicuña (vih-KOON-yuh) is especially warm and soft, making for some extra-toasty blankets! A vicuña gets a shave about every three years for farmers to collect their wool.

Easter Island is a Chilean island, which is over 2,200 miles west of the mainland, where you can find at least 600 stone statues of what look like big heads called *moai*.

ARMOR OF GOD

God's Word says His people should be "little armored ones," like armadillos! **Ephesians 6:10–18 tells us to put on the armor of God** and wear things like the belt of truth, the breastplate of righteousness, the shield of faith, and the helmet of salvation. Though these aren't literal pieces of armor, things like faith, salvation, and God's truth help protect us.

ROSEATE SPOONBILLS

The roseate spoonbill bird is named for its spoon-shaped bill. These birds look for food under shallow water, and their flat bills help them sift through the mud to find small fish, shrimp, and slugs.

FUN FACT! You can experience **Chile's temperature extremes** within a single day. You could snowboard in the cold Andes Mountains in the morning, and within three to four hours, you could be on the warm beach, ready for a surf in the sun.

CHILE

National tree

EXPLORE THE COUNTRY **Chile, which sits on the western coast of South America,** has a population of over 19 million people. Its beautiful landscape includes the Andes Mountains, the Atacama Desert, deep valleys, and the Puna grasslands. It has over 5,155 types of plants, from the Chilean pine (or monkey puzzle trees) to the Chilean fuchsia plant. It's also home to more than 400 types of birds, 150 species of mammals, and 140 kinds of reptiles!

KEY FACTS

OFFICIAL LANGUAGE: Spanish

CAPITAL CITY: Buenos Aires

NEIGHBORING COUNTRIES & BODIES OF WATER: Chile, Bolivia, Paraguay, Brazil, Uruguay, the Atlantic Ocean

NATIONAL TREE: Cockspur coral tree, also known as the ceibo (SAY-boh)

NATIONAL BIRD: Rufous hornero

NATIONAL DISH: Asado, which is barbecued meat

JOSE GABRIEL DEL ROSARIO BROCHERO

LIFESPAN: March 16, 1840– January 26, 1914

BIRTHPLACE: Santa Rosa de Río Primero, Argentina

Known as "the cowboy priest," Jose wore a poncho and sombrero and would travel across Argentina on a mule, taking care of the poor and sick.

FUN FACT! Argentina is the second-largest country in South America and the third-largest country to speak Spanish as its **primary language**.

HE IS ALIVE!

The Easter lily cactus is named for the time when it blooms—during spring around Easter time. But Easter is more than just a time to see flowers come to life. **It's the celebration of when Jesus, our Savior, was raised from the dead and overcame sin and death forever.** Now He is alive and sits at the right hand of God (1 Peter 3:22)!

PATAGONIA LANCEHEAD SNAKES

The Patagonia lancehead snake looks cool with its pointed and upturned snout, but it's best to keep this snake at a distance. It's venomous! These guys like to hang out in sandy or rocky areas but are sometimes found in forests.

Patagonia is the southernmost region of South America shared by Chile and Argentina. Only two million people live in the area (mostly within the Argentinian portion), which makes its beautiful natural landscapes mostly untouched. It includes grasslands, deserts, mountains, valleys, lakes, and glaciers, as well as incredible wildlife.

Argentinians have a high **literacy rate** of 98%, which is 12% higher than the global average. That means most people in Argentina can read and write!

PATAGONIAN HARES

The Patagonia hare keeps people guessing! While it's called a hare, it's the size of a tiny deer and actually belongs to the rodent family. It can hop and gallop and stot, which means to hop on all fours at once.

PACIFIC OCEAN

ARGENTINA

EXPLORE THE COUNTRY **Filling the southeast area of South America,** Argentina is the eighth biggest country in the world and is about one-third of the size of the United States. It is known for its fertile grasslands, where cattle roam freely across the land. In fact, the country has more cattle than people, with over 53 million cattle and 46 million people. It has more than 10,000 species of plants, 100 types of birds, 300 different species of mammals, and 55 unique species of snakes!

The first **animated movie** was made in Argentina. Released in 1917 and directed by Quirino Cristiani, the movie *El Apóstol* (*The Apostle*) is about a man who tries to become president with the help of his homemade robot, but the robot ends up taking over!

BOLIVIA

PARAGUAY

BRAZIL

CHILE

Iguazú Falls is a breathtaking waterfall, standing 269 feet tall and almost 9,000 feet wide. The falls are so gorgeous that when former first lady of the US Eleanor Roosevelt first saw them, she said, "My poor Niagara." For reference, Niagara Falls is 177 feet tall and 3,100 feet wide.

FOUR-EYED FROGS

The large four-eyed frog is a trickster! It has markings on its hind legs that also look like eyes. But these aren't just clever markings; those are poison glands to ward off anyone who gets too close!

The **cockspur coral tree** is an important symbol of bravery in Argentina. It's mentioned in many of their art forms, like poetry and songs.

Buenos Aires has the widest street in the entire world. **Avenida 9 de Julio** ("July 9th Avenue," named after the country's independence day) is 459 feet wide and has 16 lanes of traffic!

The official sport of Argentina is called **pato**. In this sport, players ride horses and try to get a rubber ball into a basket.

Argentina's grasslands, also known as the Pampas, are where Argentinians herd cattle and grow crops, like **wheat**. In fact, Argentina is one of the top 10 exporters of wheat in the whole world.

URUGUAY

★ BUENOS AIRES

CONAE (COMISIÓN NACIONAL DE ACTIVIDADES ESPACIALES)

Argentina's national space agency has launched four satellites. These satellites have been used to monitor the ocean and surrounding land to help prepare for and recover from natural disasters as well as care for natural resources.

Laguna del Carbón is a glacial (that means super cold and icy) salt lake that is known for its clear water.

ATLANTIC OCEAN

MALE PATAGONIA SEAHORSES

The male Patagonia seahorse has a brood pouch, which is where the female seahorse stores her eggs until the male gives birth to them. The average seahorse brood has about 200 baby seahorses in it, so that's one tired dad!

The **Easter lily cactus** has white and pink blooms that open at night and close during the day.

One of Argentina's 300 glaciers is one of the only glaciers in the world that is still growing: the **Perito Moreno Glacier**. This glacier covers 97 square miles and has huge ice walls!

LEARN THE LANGUAGE

INFORMAL ARGENTINIAN SPANISH

CHE (CHAY): hey; what's up?

MANGO (MAN-go): money (like saying *bucks* in the US)

MAGELLANIC PENGUINS

The largest population of Magellanic penguins is found in Argentina. They love to hang out in big groups on the beaches and swim in the cool waters of the Patagonia.

35

The world's oldest university, the **University of Karueein**, is in Fez, Morocco. It started way back in AD 859. The oldest university in Europe wasn't founded until AD 1088!

Africa is home to the world's tallest land animal. At 14 to 19 feet tall, the **giraffe** is about four times as tall as you are!

The largest animal migration (when animals travel from one location to another) is known as the **Great Migration**. Over 750,000 zebras and 1.2 million wildebeest migrate across Serengeti National Park every year.

Hippos are very aggressive toward people. They're even more dangerous than lions and tigers!

ATLANTIC OCEAN

WESTERN SAHARA

• CABO VERDE

MAURITANIA

Found in eastern and southern Africa, **cheetahs** are the world's fastest land animal, racing to speeds of 60 to 70 miles per hour.

70% of the world's **cocoa beans** (what we use to make chocolate) come from Africa, mainly from the countries Ghana, Nigeria, Cameroon, and Côte d'Ivoire.

Football (also known as soccer in the US) is the most popular sport in every African country.

THE GAMBIA

SENEGAL

GUINEA BISSAU

GUINEA

SIERRA LEONE

LIBERIA

Africa is located in the middle of the **world map**, so not only is it cut in half by the equator, but the prime meridian also crosses through Africa.

AFRICA

EXPLORE THE CONTINENT **Africa is the second-largest continent in the world!** It is home to many amazing parts of creation, like the Sahara Desert, the Nile River, and some of the coolest animals on the planet, like lions, giraffes, and cheetahs. It's also known for its many natural resources, like 30% of the whole world's mineral reserves. Divided into 54 countries, Africa has more than 3,000 different ethnic groups, and between 1,000 and 2,000 languages are spoken on the continent! It currently holds 15% of the whole world's population—about 1.2 billion people!

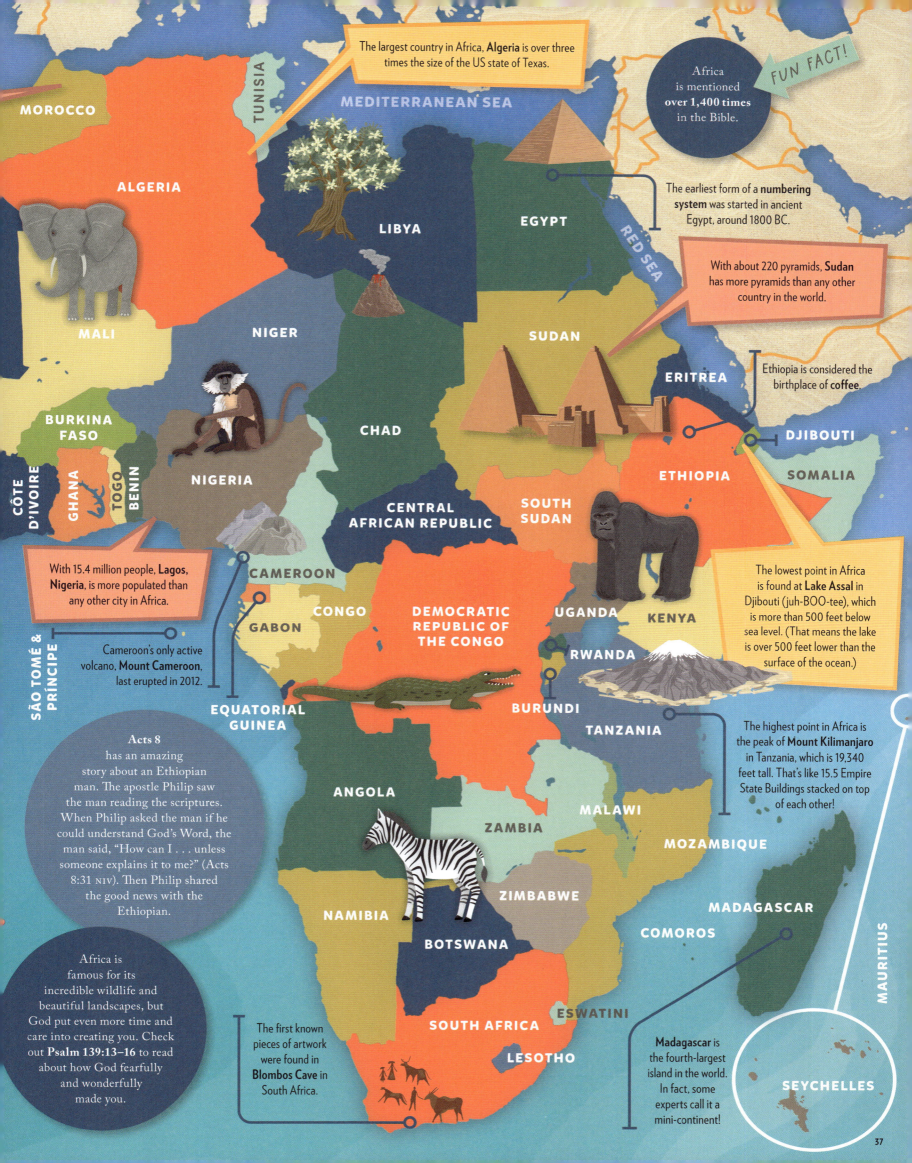

MEDITERRANEAN SEA

While most modern Egyptians are Muslim (people who follow Islam), about **10% of Egyptians are Coptic Christians**, which is one of the oldest denominations of the Christian faith.

Ancient Egyptians built the **Great Pyramids of Giza** around 2500 BC. These man-made tombs, which were created for Egyptian royalty, range from 213 to 481 feet tall. They're so big that they can even be seen from space! In fact, NASA astronauts took photos of the pyramids in 2001.

WOW!

LIBYA

Archaeologists have found around **130 pyramids** in Egypt so far.

EGYPT

The gorgeous **date palm**, which can grow up to 75 feet tall, has big, green palm leaves and bears a sweet, juicy fruit.

The Great Sphinx of Giza is one of the world's biggest sculptures at 240 feet long and 66 feet high! A sphinx is a mythical creature with a head of a man and the body of a lion.

EXPLORE THE COUNTRY Officially known as the **Arab Republic of Egypt**, this country is in the northeast corner of Africa. It's known for its deserts, low mountains, and warm temperatures, as well as its mummies, kingdom dynasties, and some of the most famous architecture in the world. And it has some crazy-cool animals, from hippopotamuses and crocodiles to camels and hyenas! Some call Egypt the "cradle of civilization" because ancient Egypt held the first communities (also known as urban centers) that developed writing, farming, organized religion, and a central government. Today, over 87 million people live in the country!

Ancient Egyptians used **hieroglyphics** to write, which used pictures and symbols to communicate.

NILE CROCODILES
The Nile crocodile can lay up to 80 eggs! And when the mama croc senses danger, she can hide her eggs in a pouch in her throat!

FUN FACT!

Egypt is mentioned in the **Bible 740 times!**

RED SPITTING COBRAS
The red spitting cobra spits venom at its prey and to scare off predators. It can hit a target eight feet away!

The **Western Desert** is so dry that it has no plant life whatsoever!

LEARN THE LANGUAGE

LISTEN TO GOD

Just because something looks cool or fun doesn't mean it's not harmful. And whether you run into a lionfish or are tempted to play a new game your parents haven't approved of, you may need help knowing what to do. But don't worry! **God sent the Holy Spirit to help us make good choices.** John 16:13 says the Holy Spirit points us to the truth. We just have to listen! You can learn the Holy Spirit's voice by reading the Bible, praying, and quietly thinking about what you read in the Bible.

SAINT ANTHONY OF EGYPT

LIFESPAN: AD 251–AD 356
BIRTHPLACE: Egypt

Known for his dedication to prayer, Anthony once lived alone on a mountain by the Nile River for 19 years, spending that time growing closer to God. He later became a teacher to other Christians near him, and he sometimes traveled to spread the gospel.

ARABIC

MIN FADLIK (min FUD-lick): please

SHUKRAN (SHOOK-rahn): thank you

SABAH ALKHAYR (sah-BAH hahl-HIE-yr): good morning

SUDAN

Bardawīl Lake is a saltwater lagoon that is 60 miles wide!

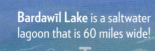 ISRAEL

KEY FACTS

CAIRO ★

The longest river in the world, the **Nile River**, is massive. It flows for over 4,000 miles and is one of the main ways Egyptian farmers get water for their crops.

NUBIAN IBEX

The Nubian Ibex lives in the mountain regions of Egypt and is famous for scaling incredibly steep cliffs.

Mount Catherine is Egypt's highest mountain, reaching an elevation of 8,668 feet. That's taller than eight Eiffel Towers stacked on top of each other.

CAMELS

Camels are made for desert life. They can store up to 80 pounds of fat in their humps, which helps them survive for a long time without food or water. They can even drink 40 gallons of water in one sitting!

Egypt doesn't get much **rain**. In fact, the city of Cairo gets less than an inch a year!

LIONFISH

Found in the coral reefs in the Red Sea, the lionfish is one of the more dangerous creatures in Egypt. The spines on its back contain one of the deadliest venoms in the world!

OFFICIAL LANGUAGE: Arabic

CAPITAL CITY: Cairo

NEIGHBORING COUNTRIES & BODIES OF WATER: Libya, Mediterranean Sea, Israel, Red Sea, Sudan

NATIONAL TREE: Doum palm

NATIONAL BIRD: Steppe eagle

NATIONAL DISH: Koshari (sometimes spelled *koshary* or *kushari*), a mix of lentils, macaroni noodles, and rice, covered with a spicy tomato sauce with Middle Eastern spices, garbanzo beans, and onions

RED SEA

 SAUDI ARABIA

Pharaohs were the rulers of ancient Egypt. It meant they were in charge of the people, the government, and religion, just like a king. Check out Exodus 5–12 in the Bible to see Moses face the Pharaoh and demand that he free God's people, the Israelites, from slavery—just as God said to.

Egypt's **Eastern Desert** doesn't get much rainfall, but it still has some amazing plants. You can find acacia (ah-KAY-sha) trees, a tree without leaves or thorns called a *markh* (mark), shrubs, small succulents, and even some herbs.

DR. HILANA SEDAROUS

LIFESPAN: 1904–1998

BIRTHPLACE: Tanta, Egypt

Dr. Sedarous became a doctor in 1930. She was the first female Coptic Christian doctor in Egypt. She worked in surgery at a Coptic hospital in Cairo, but she also opened her own clinic that focused on women's health.

In **Matthew 2:13–15**, Mary and Joseph left their home, family, and friends and took their newborn baby, Jesus, to live in Egypt. They probably felt unsettled and lonely at times—because moving to a new place can be tough! How can you help new kids in your neighborhood and school feel welcome? What can you do to share the love of Christ with them? Share kind words with them to help them feel more at home in a new place!

ABYSSINIAN CATS

Abyssinian cats are long, skinny, and athletic. They're famous for looking like the statutes the ancient Egyptians made.

39

SAHARA DESERT

The highest point in the Sahara is **Emi Koussi**, a volcano found in Chad. Emi Koussi reaches a whopping 11,204 feet high. Scientists don't know when it last erupted, but there are still some thermal (or hot) areas found on the south side of the volcano!

The **sand dunes in the Sahara can reach up to 600 feet high!**

WOW!

Matthew 4 tells us how Jesus spent 40 days wandering in the wilderness without any food or water. It may have felt like He was walking through the sandy dunes of the Sahara on some days! Though He was tired, hungry, and thirsty, Jesus spent His time praying. **And even when Satan tempted Him to disobey God, Jesus stayed faithful.**

The lowest point in the Sahara is the **Qattara** (ka-TAR-ah) **Depression** in Egypt. (A depression is where the land has sunken down deep.) It sits at 436 feet below sea level.

The Sahara Desert **crosses 10 countries**: Algeria, Chad, Egypt, Libya, Mali, Mauritania, Morocco, Niger, Sudan, and Tunisia.

Some desert plants store water inside of them so they can survive long periods of time with no rain. We may experience our own kind of "drought" when we feel distant from others and from God. **But God has given us His Word to store inside us to make it through hard times.** Just check out Psalm 119:11: "I have hidden your word in my heart that I might not sin against you" (NIV).

Saharan cheetahs are nocturnal, which means they only go out at night. This helps them survive by avoiding the extreme heat during the day.

The **wild desert gourd** is a member of the watermelon family. Because its leaves and fruits store water, it doesn't need much rainfall. And it's a perfect snack for hungry animals passing by—that is, if they're strong enough to break the gourd's hard rind!

Plants in the Sahara have pretty cool ways to survive without much water. After a rainfall, some herbs sprout out of the ground, bloom, and then drop their seeds to create more plants within the span of a week or two! They're called **ephemerals** (eh-FEM-er-als), which means they don't last long!

EXPLORE THE ECOSYSTEM

The Sahara Desert covers most of the northern part of Africa, spanning 3,000 miles from east to west. About a quarter of the Sahara has flat sand and tall hills of sand called sand dunes, but that's not all you can find in this wonder of creation. It is also home to tall mountains, flat plateaus, deep valleys, salt flats (areas of land that look like layers of sand or snow but are actually salt), sand- and gravel-covered plains, and 20 lakes. It's the most famous desert in the world, and you've probably seen people riding camels across it in movies.

The Sahara Desert is one of the best places on Earth to see our galaxy, the **Milky Way**. Because there are fewer city lights, the land and sky get very dark at night. This means the thick band of stars shines brightly, creating beautiful swirls of color.

The **pharaoh eagle owls** have cute little faces, orange-colored eyes, and soft tufts of feathers on their ears, but they are serious hunters! Their wings are completely silent while they're flying, so they can easily sneak up on their prey.

When the sun is up, the **temperature** usually raises to 100 degrees Fahrenheit, but it drops to about 25 degrees Fahrenheit at night. That's almost 10 degrees colder than the temperature at which water freezes, 32 degrees Fahrenheit!

Camels are built for life in the Sahara. To make sure sand doesn't get in their eyes, God made them with three eyelids and two rows of eyelashes! They can even close their nostrils completely during a sandstorm.

About half of the land in the Sahara gets **less than an inch of rain** each year!

Camels are so important to the residents of the Sahara that the Arabic language has over **160 words** for camel.

The **Laperrine olive tree** is so tough that it can grow tall and produce olives even during the most extreme drought.

When you think of a **desert**, you probably picture a hot, dry, sandy place. But a **desert** is any area of land that gets less than 10 inches of rain a year. The two biggest deserts in the world are actually cold, located in the Arctic and Antarctica. The Sahara is the third-largest desert in the world and the largest hot desert.

The **deathstalker scorpion** lives up to its scary name—its toxic venom makes it one of the deadliest scorpions in the world. This predator may be only four inches long, but its tail can strike its prey at 51 inches per second, or three miles an hour! That's incredibly fast for such a little guy.

Fennec foxes may be the smallest fox species in the world, but their six-inch bat-like ears radiate, or fan out, their body heat to keep them cool. Their thick fur keeps them cool during the day and warm at night and protects their feet from getting burned on the hot sand.

The Sahara might be a pretty dry place, but you can still find some sources of water! Both the **Nile** and the **Niger Rivers** flow through it.

GHANA

MALI

BURKINA FASO

AWESOME! Ghana is home to many artists. They are known for their sculpting, cloth weaving, and wood carving and use skills passed down through generations. Villages that focus on creating these beautiful, traditional pieces of art are known as craft villages, and they're famous around the world!

PATAS MONKEYS
The adorable patas monkeys spend most of their time on the ground rather than high in the trees like other species of monkeys.

MONGOOSES
Mongooses live in the forests of Ghana. They may seem cuddly, but these ferret-looking creatures are known to start fights with the black mamba—one of the most venomous snakes in Africa. But don't worry! Mongooses have a natural immunity to snake venom. So those snakes better watch out!

Two-thirds of Ghana is covered in **savanna**, a grassy plain with a few short trees.

EXPLORE THE COUNTRY
Sitting on the Gulf of Guinea in West Africa, this small country is 92,000 square miles, making it slightly smaller than the state of Oregon. It is home to beautiful savannas—flat, hot, grassy areas—and beaches and forests. Ghana has over 32 million people and at least 75 spoken languages. It's one of the first countries south of the Sahara to become an independent country!

CÔTE D'IVOIRE

Ghana is home to the **Mole National Park**, a place that protects elephants from harm and where tourists can come face-to-face with these gentle giants.

Ghana has **a tropical climate**, which means the temperatures are almost always warm. In fact, the temperature in Ghana's capital city of Accra rarely dips below 73 degrees Fahrenheit.

The **baobab** (BOW-bab) tree stores water in its trunk and produces a fruit packed with nutrients. It's a great source of food during the dry season when other plants might've died. That's why it's called the "Tree of Life."

The primary **religion** in Ghana is Christianity.

The **Kwahu Plateau** stretches for 160 miles. A plateau is an area of level high ground that's often surrounded by steep, rocky slopes.

LEARN THE LANGUAGE

TWI LANGUAGE
Twi is the language spoken by 85% of the Ghanaian population.

MEDASSE (muh-DAH-see): thank you

MEM A WO AKYE (mem ah woe AAH-cheh): good morning

DA YIE (da YEE-ay): good night

NYAME ADOM (nye-AH-me aa-DOHM): by the grace of God

DAVID ASANTE
LIFESPAN: 1834–1892
BIRTHPLACE: Akropong, Ghana

David was one of the first people to translate the Bible into the Twi language. He also mastered German, Greek, Latin, and Hebrew and later was ordained as a Lutheran pastor.

The **rainforests** in Ghana used to be around 30,000 square miles, but they've been getting smaller and only around 8,000 square miles are left. But there's good news! About 6,000 miles of the rainforests are protected, which means there are rules against cutting down the trees in that area.

If you want to see the jungle from a bird's point of view, check out the **Kakum Canopy Walkway**. It's a series of rope and wire bridges that hang about 130 feet above the jungle floor and cover over 1,000 feet of the jungle!

Ghana's west coast gets up to **80 inches of rain** each year. That's the same height as a line of 10 and a half pencils.

42

BUTTERFLIES
Nearly 1,000 species of butterflies flutter across Ghana.

BENIN

AFRICAN SNAILS
Ghana is one of the only places you can see the giant African snail in the wild. They are about seven inches long and considered to be a great source of protein.

CLEMENT ANDERSON AKROFI

LIFESPAN: 1901–1967

BIRTHPLACE: Apirede, Ghana

Clement spent years studying his own language, Twi. He eventually revised the Twi Bible so that others could read and better understand God's Word for themselves.

KEY FACTS

OFFICIAL LANGUAGE: English

CAPITAL CITY: Accra

NEIGHBORING COUNTRIES & BODIES OF WATER: Côte d'Ivoire, Burkina Faso, Togo, the Gulf of Guinea

NATIONAL TREE: Big Tree (the tallest tree in West Africa, located near the city of Akim Oda)

NATIONAL BIRD: Tawny eagle

NATIONAL DISH: *Fufu*, a side dish made by pounding unripe plantains and cassava (the starchy root of a tropical tree) with a big wooden pole while mixing in water; once the dough is mixed, it is rolled into balls and served with stews and soups

AFRICAN CIVETS
African civets are nocturnal mammals, which means they are awake at night and sleep during the day. They're pretty relaxed critters—except when they run into lions, hyenas, or leopards!

TOGO

Lake Volta is one of the largest man-made bodies of water in the world, and many Ghanaians use it for travel or to send or receive supplies. That's a pretty important body of water! But no water on Earth can compare to the Living Water. The Living Water isn't man-made, but it does come from a man—Jesus, the Son of God. Jesus said, "Whoever drinks the water I give will never be thirsty again. The water I give will become a spring of water flowing inside him. It will give him eternal life" (John 4:14 ICB).

THE GHANA SPACE SCIENCE AND TECHNOLOGY INSTITUTE
The **Ghana Space Science and Technology Institute** uses satellites that orbit the Earth to capture images of Ghana. Those images help the country forecast the weather, discover changes in their land and coastline, and solve problems during natural disasters, like earthquakes or fires, so they can help people as quickly as possible.

SPEND TIME WITH GOD

In 2021, Ghana was ranked as the **second most peaceful country** in Africa! But as Christians, we don't need to be in a certain place to have peace—even when times are tough. Why? Because when we spend time with God, He fills us with peace. Check out John 16:33 and Isaiah 26:3 to find these promises!

ANTS
In the coastal savannas around the city of Accra, ants build giant anthills up to 14 feet tall!

★ ACCRA

NIGERIA

HUMPBACK WHALES
Humpback whales can be spotted in the Gulf of Guinea near the city of Takoradi between the months of July and December. They weigh up to 40 tons. That's about 80,000 pounds!

BEAUTIFUL!

Ghana is famous for a textile (a type of fabric) known as kente (KEN-tay). **Kente cloth is a beautiful, handwoven cloth made of rich, vibrant colors like black, green, red, and gold.** Legend has it that two men learned to weave by watching a spider weave a web.

GULF OF GUINEA

At 1,000 miles long, the main river system in Ghana is the **Volta River**, which is mainly made up of the Black and White Volta Rivers. They flow south through the country into the Gulf of Guinea.

ATLANTIC OCEAN

KEY FACTS

OFFICIAL LANGUAGE: English

CAPITAL CITY: Abuja

NEIGHBORING COUNTRIES & BODIES OF WATER: Benin, Niger, Chad, Cameroon, the Gulf of Guinea

NATIONAL TREE: Camphor tree

NATIONAL BIRD: Black-crowned crane

NATIONAL DISH: Jollof rice, a spicy, flavorful rice dish that is cooked in broth with tomatoes, peppers, and herbs

AARDVARKS
Aardvarks look like a cross between a pig, an armadillo, and a rodent. These critters tend to live alone and use their strong claws to make underground burrows. In fact, they're such excellent diggers that they can move two feet of soil in 15 seconds!

FAITH
The **two major religions** in Nigeria are Islam and Christianity: 50% of Nigerians are Muslim and 48% are Christians.

Hippos may look cute and harmless, but they're actually very dangerous—and super-fast! Thankfully, you probably won't face a hippo anytime soon, but you might find another kind of "hippo" in your life. Sometimes sin can look harmless, but it's not. So what should you do? **Take time every day to read the Bible, pray, and ask God to lead you away from anything that is not good for you.**

HIPPOS
Hippos are chatterboxes, talking with one another through honks, squeaks, and whines that you can hear almost 1.5 miles away!

GALAGOS
Bush babies, also known as galagos (guh-LAY-goz), might be the cutest critters out there. They have big round eyes and love to move around by jumping. They may look like squirrels, but they're actually primates, the same as monkeys!

ABUJA

The Federal University of Technology Akure created the Nigeria EduSat-1, the first satellite built in Nigeria, with a special mission—to get people interested in space! Operators sent audio files of popular songs to the satellite, which would transmit, or send, the songs back to Earth using radio waves. Kids could use handheld radios to find the signal from the satellite—and hear the songs!

BENIN

The roots of the **mangrove trees** appear above ground, making them look like they're standing above water. They're usually found on coastlines, so their tangle of roots makes a good home for fish who want to hide from predators.

In June 2017, **Nigeria EduSat-1** launched into space—but not from the ground. This cube-shaped instrument made its debut into the cosmos from the International Space Station!

Modern Nigerians love football (also known as soccer in the US). Their national team is called the Super Eagles, and they even won a gold medal at the 1996 Olympics!

NIGERIA

RED COLOBUS MONKEYS
The red colobus monkeys, which are found near the Niger Delta, are the most endangered monkeys in Africa. There are only about 500 left on the entire planet!

EXPLORE THE COUNTRY
With over 222 million people, Nigeria is the most populated country in Africa and the sixth most populated country in the world. It represents more than 300 people groups (including the Hausa, Yoruba, and Igbo) and 500 languages! Its land spreads across 356 square miles, making it larger than the state of Texas. This west African country is mostly flat with a few hills and plateaus and is filled with interesting animals, from hyenas to baboons!

GULF OF GUINEA

CHAD

Lake Chad is a large freshwater lake found in Nigeria, Chad, Cameroon, and Niger. After heavy rainfall, the surface of the lake can get up to 920 feet above sea level. The lake is surrounded by beautiful plants, like desert date trees and African myrrh.

NIGER

BLACK-CROWNED CRANES

The black-crowned crane has an inflatable pouch under its chin that it uses to make loud booming noises.

A man named **Christopher Alexander Sapara Williams** became the first Nigerian lawyer. He also regularly spoke out against slavery.

Most of the country is covered with savannas (flat, grassy areas).

The Jos Plateau in Nigeria is an area of flat, raised earth that covers about 3,000 square miles and is 4,200 feet high. And while the area might be a great place for people to live now, that wasn't always the case. The plateau is on top of several extinct volcanoes!

PUFF ADDER SNAKES

Don't mess with the puff adder! This venomous snake is responsible for the most snakebite deaths in all of Africa.

SAMUEL AJAYI CROWTHER

LIFESPAN: c. 1809–December 31, 1891

BIRTHPLACE: Nigeria

Originally from the Yoruba region in Nigeria, Samuel was enslaved around the age of 12, then set free 15 years later. He soon became a Christian and wanted to spend his time sharing the gospel with others. He became a bishop (a church minister) in the Church Missionary Society in 1864, the first African to have this high position in the Anglican Church!

FUN FACT!

Music and dance are huge parts of modern Nigerian culture, and each people group in Nigeria uses dance and music in their own unique way. For instance, dancers from the Ishan people in Nigeria dress in colorful outfits and dance on stilts. Ubakala people use dance to fix disagreements between people, make changes within the community, and even talk about morals.

IBADAN MALIMBES

The Ibadan malimbe (ee-BAH-dihn mah-LIM-bay)  is known for the bright red feathers on its head and the unique songs that it chirps, which are made of high-pitched wheezing and swizzling-like noises. It sounds like *chup-ee-wurr*. Give it a try!

CROSS RIVER GORILLAS

The Cross River gorillas live in the mountains between Nigeria and Cameroon by the—you guessed it—Cross River. About 300 of the gorillas live in this region, which is about 3,000 square miles. (That's two times bigger than Rhode Island.) The Cross River gorillas are almost extinct, but many people are working to save the species.

Nigeria contains a portion of the **Cross-Sanaga-Bioko forests**, one of the wettest places in Africa, which means it's the home to a lot of different animal life, like the Cross River lowland gorilla, the Bibundi bat, and the pitch shrew.

CAMEROON

The **southeast region** has a hot and wet climate. It gets more than 120 inches of rain each year!

LEARN THE LANGUAGE

IGBO

Igbo is a language spoken primarily in the southeastern part of Nigeria.

NDEWO (n-DAY-wuh): hello

NNOO (naw): welcome

BIKO (BEE-koh): please

REJOICE!

Nigerians are often called the most optimistic people on earth. That means Nigerians tend to be happy and look on the bright side of things. How amazing is that? And while we can't always be happy, the Bible says that Christians should always rejoice (which means to celebrate) in the Lord. Try memorizing this verse to remind yourself to find happiness in Christ on hard days: "Rejoice in the Lord always. I will say it again: Rejoice!" (Philippians 4:4 NIV).

45

CHARLES LWANGA

LIFESPAN: 1865–June 3, 1886

BIRTHPLACE: Buganda (now Uganda)

Charles became a Christian early in life after meeting Catholic missionaries in his village. When he was older, he was put in charge of the king's servants, and he shared the good news about Jesus with them. The king ordered Charles to give up his Christian beliefs, but Charles refused and remained faithful to God.

SOUTH SUDAN

ETHIOPIA

Uganda is the home to one of the **world's smallest churches**. Located on Biku Hill, it's eight feet tall and eight feet wide, and it can only fit three people inside—including the pastor!

FAITH

More than 85% of Kenyans are Christian. Another 11% are Muslim, and 2% believe in other religions, like Hinduism, Sikhism, and the Bahá'í Faith.

ELEPHANT SHREWS

Elephant shrews get their name from their long snouts, but unlike elephants, they're only about 12 inches long. Even though they are tiny, they can jump three feet in the air in a single hop!

SHOEBILL STORKS

The shoebill stork might look silly with its big beak, but it's one brave bird! It's not afraid to fight other creatures, even Nile crocodiles!

The **Murchison Falls National Park** offers visitors a chance to see the Big Five—the lion, leopard, rhino, elephant, and buffalo—as well as a gorgeous waterfall that is 140 feet tall!

DEMOCRATIC REPUBLIC OF THE CONGO

LAKE ALBERT

WARTHOGS

Warthogs love to sleep in holes to keep cool after a long day in the sun. And although they can dig holes themselves, they usually choose ones already dug by other animals, like aardvarks. It makes life a little easier after a hard day's work of eating grass, bulbs, and roots.

Uganda is home to the **Rwenzori mountains**. The highest peak in the mountain range, Margherita Peak, is over 16,000 feet tall!

Uganda's first satellite, **PearlAfricaSat-1**, was launched into space from the International Space Station on December 2, 2022. Created by three Ugandan engineers, this satellite will help the country learn more about its weather conditions and natural disasters.

★ **KAMPALA**

Rwenzori Mountains National Park is the perfect place for bird watchers. It's the home to 217 species of birds, including rancolins and strange weavers.

LAKE VICTORIA

RWANDA

Lake Victoria is Africa's largest freshwater lake and measures 210 miles from the north end to the south end.

UGANDA

FAITH

Over 80% of Ugandans are Christian, and 14% are Muslim.

EXPLORE THE COUNTRY **With over 45 million people,** this eastern African country has three main people groups (the Baganda, Banyankole, and the Basoga people) and represents 40 native languages. It's a beautiful landscape that spans across a large plateau, is filled with lakes and rivers, and is surrounded by mountains. It's also teeming with life and has over 350 mammal species alone, from gorillas to rhinoceroses to bats!

TANZANIA

KENYA

PULL TOGETHER

The Kenyan motto of *harambee* (ha-rum-BAY) means "to pull together." **It encourages people from different backgrounds to create one community and care for one another.** The Bible talks about this too! Hebrews 10:24–25 and 1 Corinthians 1:10 encourage us to stick together, love each other, and have peace among us. What are ways that you can "pull together" with your friends and family?

GREVY ZEBRAS
The Grevy zebra is the largest of all zebra species, growing up to five feet tall. Their large ears and reddish-brown stripes that darken to black over time also make them stand out against other striped pals.

EXPLORE THE COUNTRY
With over 50 million people, Kenya represents more than 40 different people groups (including the Kikuyu, Luhya, and Kalenjin) and 70 languages. The equator runs through this eastern African country, giving it a hot and humid climate that helps some incredible plants grow—like cedar trees, bamboo, and short grasses. Kenya has low plains near its coastline that rise into plateaus and mountains in the center of the country. It's the perfect spot for some of the world's most amazing animals, from zebras to ostriches to warthogs!

The Great Rift Valley is a ridge system, which means that over the years the ground shifted and moved apart, creating deep rifts or canyons. The Great Rift Valley runs north to south through Kenya and is full of active volcanoes, geysers, and hot springs!

This **large buffalo and tiny bird** are very different animals. Yet they were created by God to help one another. It's a great example of how God created everything on purpose and with a purpose.

CAPE BUFFALO
Cape buffalo are unlikely best friends with a tiny species of bird known as oxpeckers. You can usually spot these little guys perched on a buffalo's back, snacking on ticks and other bugs on the ox's skin.

Kenya's highest peak is **Mount Kenya,** which stands at 17,058 feet. That's as tall as 1,300 elephants stacked on top of each other!

CHEETAHS VS. LEOPARDS
Cheetahs and leopards might look similar, but they don't act the same. While a cheetah will run after its prey, a leopard hunts by tracking its prey and sneaking up on it with a stealthy pounce.

★ NAIROBI
You probably won't put on an astronaut suit and head into space anytime soon. But you can go to space camp! **The Kenya Space Agency** created a space camp to share all the latest information on robots, rockets, planets, and how we can use satellites in space to help us take care of Earth.

ESAU KHAMATI SAMBAYI ORIEDO
LIFESPAN: January 29, 1888– December 1, 1992
BIRTHPLACE: Bunyore, Kenya

Esau was a Christian evangelist (someone who preaches the gospel) in Kenya. He also fought for the right for free education, which led to Kenya's first official school.

FUN FACT!
Family is incredibly important to Kenyans. Many Kenyans grow up closely with not just their parents and siblings but also their aunts, uncles, grandparents, and cousins. It's a normal custom for the whole family to get together for a delicious dinner.

The Maasai people in Kenya are **experts at beading**. They use colorful beaded jewelry, like necklaces, to show a person's social status or life stage.

KEY FACTS

OFFICIAL LANGUAGES: Swahili and English

CAPITAL CITY
UGANDA: Kampala
KENYA: Nairobi

NEIGHBORING COUNTRIES & BODIES OF WATER:
UGANDA: Democratic Republic of the Congo, South Sudan, Kenya, Tanzania, Rwanda, Lake Victoria
KENYA: Tanzania, Uganda, South Sudan, Ethiopia, Somalia, Indian Ocean, Lake Victoria

NATIONAL BIRD
UGANDA: Gray-crowned crane
KENYA: Lilac-breasted roller

INDIAN OCEAN

NAMIBIA

EXPLORE THE COUNTRY Namibia has 11 people groups who speak over 30 languages, with a total population of 2.5 million. The country is sparsely populated, meaning there is a lot of open land. Namibia's landscape includes deserts, plateaus, mountains, and grassy plains, which are perfect for the large animal population that roams freely across the country, from giraffes to kudus to meerkats!

ATLANTIC OCEAN

ANGOLA

WILD HORSES
Though no one knows how they got there, wild horses have lived on the eastern edge of the Namib Desert for more than 100 years.

MEERKATS
Meerkats are social creatures and live in large family groups. You can find them in the Kalahari and Namib Deserts.

The Etosha Pan is a large salt flat that glimmers green during the dry season. The region was formed when a lake dried up, leaving behind a large area of land topped with the salt that didn't evaporate.

FAITH
About 80% of Namibians are Christian, and the other 20% believe in Animism.

TENEBRIONID BEETLES
On foggy mornings in the Namib Desert, tenebrionid beetles crawl to the top of sand dunes and stand on their heads to snatch a little drink from the fog as it settles.

★ WINDHOEK
Namibia was the landing site to the **Gibeon meteorite shower**, one of the most intense meteorite showers ever. To date, scientists have discovered around 120 pieces of meteorites (or space rocks) that weighed nearly 25 tons. (That's as heavy as 12.5 cars!) You can still see some of the meteorites on display in Namibia's capital.

The Skeleton Coast is a region of massive sand dunes that reach up to 300 feet high. It might sound spooky, but the Skeleton Coast is named for the many abandoned wrecked ships and animal bones found there.

One of Namibia's people groups is called the **Himba**. They're a nomadic people, which means they move from place to place instead of living in one location. They don't interact with people outside their ethnic group often.

The **Namib Desert** holds some of the driest regions in the whole world. But the lack of water doesn't scare off some rodents. The dune hairy-footed gerbil and Grant's golden mole both make their homes in this desert.

KUDUS
Kudus are a type of antelope with long, spiraled antlers. But the fancy horns don't mean they want attention. Kudus are shy and are more likely to run away than stand and fight when approached.

KEY FACTS

OFFICIAL LANGUAGES
NAMIBIA: English
BOTSWANA: English and Setswana
ZIMBABWE: Chewa, Chibarwe, English, Kalanga, Khoisan, Nambya, Ndau, Ndebele, Shangani, Shona, sign language, Sotho, Tonga, Tswana, Venda, and Xhosa

CAPITAL CITY
NAMIBIA: Windhoek
BOTSWANA: Gaborone
ZIMBABWE: Harare

NATIONAL TREE
NAMIBIA: Quiver tree
BOTSWANA: Marula
ZIMBABWE: Big Tree in Chirinda Forest

NATIONAL BIRD
NAMIBIA: African fish eagle
BOTSWANA: Kori bustard
ZIMBABWE: Zimbabwe bird (a stone-carved bird representing the bateleur eagle)

ZIMBABWE

ZAMBIA

The **Zimbezi River** is home to a lot of wildlife, including hippopotamuses and crocodiles! Did you know that crocodiles can have twice as many teeth as humans? That's up to 60 teeth!

EXPLORE THE COUNTRY
Zimbabwe spans across mostly flat, grassy land. With 15 million people and 16 different languages, Zimbabwe is known for its diversity in cultures, as well as in animals and plants. The rich plant growth includes the bush lily, mango tree, and sago palm plant. And many incredible animals make their home in this breathtaking country, from antelopes to crocodiles to African wild dogs.

Botswana is serious about **keeping their wildlife protected**, with 40% of the land dedicated to national parks or wildlife preservations.

Victoria Falls, the biggest waterfall in the world, is one of the greatest natural wonders in all of Africa. Its traditional name is Mosi-oa-Tunya, which means "smoke that thunders." And the huge amount of water that pours over the falls certainly thunders. You can hear the water crashing from 25 miles away!

★ HARARE

Zimbabwe has many species of Brachystegia (BRACK-uh-STEE-juh) trees, which have reddish-brown wood. These trees can grow up to 90 feet tall. That's as tall as a nine-story building!

IMPALAS
Impalas may not run fast, but they can jump over nine feet high. And when a predator like a wild dog comes close, the impala herd scatters in different directions, hoping to confuse the attacker and get to safety.

GIRAFFES
Giraffes stick to the bushlands in the western region of the country, where they eat their favorite food, leaves from acacia (ah-KAY-sha) trees! In one day, they can eat 75 pounds of food.

Botswana's **blady grass** can grow up to 10 feet tall and can be weaved into mats or used to build roofs.

MOZAMBIQUE

ELEPHANTS
More elephants live in Botswana than in any country, with about 130,000 elephants stomping across the land.

★ GABORONE

Botswana's **savanna** has tall yellow and light-brown grass, acacia (ah-KAY-sha) shrubs, and several types of trees.

ANDIMBA TOIVO YA TOIVO
LIFESPAN: August 22, 1924–June 9, 2017
BIRTHPLACE: Namibia

Andimba dedicated his life to fighting for freedom. He spoke out against unfair South African rulers in Namibia, and he even spent time in prison with another activist calling for change, Nelson Mandela.

SOUTH AFRICA

BOTSWANA

AWESOME
Millions of people have visited Botswana to see the amazing landscapes and stunning wildlife. But even if you don't plan to visit anytime soon, setting aside time to appreciate nature is important for everyone to do. Why? Because it reminds us that creation has a Creator (Romans 1:20). **So take a moment to appreciate all that God has made!**

EXPLORE THE COUNTRY
Almost 2.5 million people live in Botswana. While this country is home to several people groups, the largest is the Tswana (SWAH-nuh) people, which makes up 80% of the population. There are also more than 20 languages spoken throughout the country. Botswana has a mostly flat landscape, which is a perfect foundation for growing plants, like the sycamore fig tree, the baobab (BOW-bab) tree, and blady grass. You'll also find some incredible wildlife here, from the gnu to the bee-eater bird to the impala.

SOUTH AFRICA

EXPLORE THE COUNTRY
South Africa is at the southernmost tip of the continent of Africa. It has a population of more than 60 million people and has 11 official languages, including Afrikaans, English, and Zulu. It also has 21 national parks and is known for its amazing plant and animal life, including 20,000 types of flowers, more than 800 species of birds, 100 types of snakes, and so much more! In fact, millions of people visit South Africa every year and enjoy the world-famous safaris that show off its beautiful land, animals, and plants.

MIRIAM MAKEBA
LIFESPAN: March 4, 1932– November 10, 2008
BIRTHPLACE: Johannesburg, South Africa
Miriam was a world-famous singer who got her start singing in church.

SOMEDAY!
South Africa's savanna is full of ferocious animals. If you see a lion, keep your distance to stay safe! But God says heaven won't be this way. Isaiah 11:6 explains it like this: "In that day the wolf and the lamb will live together; the leopard will lie down with the baby goat. The calf and the yearling will be safe with the lion, and a little child will lead them all" (NLT).
Someday we'll enjoy peace with everyone—even the animals!

NAMIBIA

LEOPARDS
Leopards are the strongest climbers of all big cats. They can carry prey twice their own weight up a tree.

ELEPHANTS
An African elephant's ears are shaped like the continent of Africa.

ATLANTIC OCEAN

At 1,367 miles, the **Orange River** is the longest river in the country.

The **plateau**, an area of level high ground, covers about two-thirds of the country.

SALT
The **South African Large Telescope** (SALT) is made up of 91 hexagonal mirrors and is the biggest telescope in the whole southern hemisphere. It's taken beautiful images of a galaxy called NGC 6744, which is 30 million light years away!

The **Succulent Karoo** is a region in South Africa's desert lands known for its rich and diverse plant life, including, of course, succulents.

LEARN THE LANGUAGE

AFRIKAANS
OLIFANT (OH-lih-funt): elephant

BUFFEL (buff-el): buffalo

GRASVELD (GRASS-veld): grassland

PLATO (PLAH-toh): plateau

LUIPERD (LY-purd): leopard

ZULU
INDLOVU (EEND-lo-voo): elephant

INYATHI (in-YEH-tee): buffalo

★ CAPE TOWN

AFRICAN PENGUINS
Not all penguins need the cold and ice! These guys make their home in the coastal waters of South Africa, where the temperatures range from 41–68 degrees Fahrenheit.

ZIMBABWE

At 4.9 million acres, **Kruger National Park** is the largest wildlife sanctuary in the country, home to the Big Five (lions, leopards, elephants, African buffalo, and rhinoceroses).

RHINOCEROSES
Both the black and white rhinoceros were near extinction. But thanks to organizations that work to conserve, or protect, these creatures, the population has jumped from 2,400 in 1995 to 5,600 in 2022.

BOTSWANA

The **South African bushveld** is known for its shrubs, trees, and tall grasses and plants. It's one of the few places in the world where rare black rhinoceroses and cheetahs live.

LIONS
A lion's family unit is called a pride, which is a group of about two to three males, five to 10 females, and their cubs.

★ **PRETORIA**

BUFFALO
The African buffalo males spar with each other to determine who's boss. In fact, the place where their long horns fuse together on the top of their heads is called a *boss*.

ESWATINI

★ **BLOEMFONTEIN**

Antelope, white rhinos, elephants, and wildebeest munch on **70 kinds of grass**.

LESOTHO

Lesotho is completely surrounded by South Africa.

The **rainy season**, which lasts from October to April, provides most areas with 75% of its annual rainfall.

FAITH
About **84%** of the population identifies as Christian. Dutch missionaries went to South Africa in the 1600s, but the stories of Jesus could have reached the people even earlier!

The **Great Escarpment** is made of the steep slopes that run from the plateau down toward the ocean.
The Zulu people call the Great Escarpment the "barrier of pointed spears" for the jagged points of the mountain peaks.

KEY FACTS

OFFICIAL LANGUAGE: South Africa has 11 official languages, but English is most widely used for business

CAPITAL CITIES: Pretoria, Cape Town, Bloemfontein

NEIGHBORING COUNTRIES & BODIES OF WATER: Botswana, Mozambique, Namibia, Eswatini, Lesotho, Zimbabwe, Indian Ocean, Atlantic Ocean

NATIONAL TREE: Real yellowwood

NATIONAL BIRD: Blue crane

NATIONAL DISH: Bobotie, a casserole made of minced lamb or beef mixed with curry powder, herbs, spices, and dried fruit, then topped with milk and egg that bakes into a delicious crust

FUN FACT: If you're in South Africa, you'll likely hear some **jazz, pop,** or **Christian choral music**.

INDIAN OCEAN

About a decade apart, each of these men won the Nobel Peace Prize for helping their government get rid of unjust laws.

NELSON MANDELA
LIFESPAN: July 18, 1918–December 5, 2013
BIRTHPLACE: Mvezo, South Africa

Known as the "father of modern South Africa," Nelson was president of South Africa from 1994–1999. While speaking at a conference, he said, "The Good News [was] borne by our risen Messiah who chose not one race, who chose not one country, who chose not one language, who chose not one tribe, who chose all of humankind!"

DESMOND TUTU
LIFESPAN: October 7, 1931–December 26, 2021
BIRTHPLACE: Klerksdorp, South Africa

Desmond, who is known as "South Africa's moral conscience," wanted to be a doctor, but he studied to be a teacher. Then he was called by God to become a priest.

EUROPE

Iceland, one of the **last places on Earth to be settled** by humans, is found in Europe. Vikings discovered the region known as Iceland over 1,000 years ago!

ICELAND

Iceland **doesn't have mosquitos**, largely due to the cold temperatures and having little standing water to attract them.

NORTH SEA

IRELAND

UNITED KINGDOM

EXPLORE THE CONTINENT

Europe is the second-smallest continent on Earth and home of 44 different countries. Over 742 million people live in Europe, with over 200 languages spoken there. Many languages spoken fall into three big groups: Romance Languages (like French, Spanish, and Italian), Germanic Languages (like German, Dutch, Norwegian, and Swedish), and Slavic Languages (like Russian, Ukrainian, and Czech). But Europe is home to more than just people: 270 species of mammals and 75 species of amphibians live there!

Belgium is **famous for its chocolate**, but you might be surprised to learn where most visitors stock up on their favorite Belgian chocolate: the airport! More Belgian chocolate is sold at the Brussels Airport than anywhere else in the world!

BELGIUM

FRANCE

Around 39% of Europe is **farmland**.

Several countries in Europe have a **monarchy** (a government ruled by a king or queen): Spain, Sweden, Norway, the Netherlands, Belgium, Monaco, Luxembourg, Liechtenstein, Andorra, Denmark, Vatican City, and the United Kingdom.

PORTUGAL

SPAIN

ANDORRA

MONACO

The **Alps** are the longest and highest mountain range found entirely in Europe, and the highest peak of the Alps is Mount Blanc, which is on the border of Italy and France.

ATLANTIC OCEAN

Italy is referenced throughout the New Testament and is the country where **Paul wrote several books of the Bible**, including Ephesians, Philippians, Colossians, Philemon, and 2 Timothy.

PORTUGAL

EXPLORE THE COUNTRY

Situated between the Atlantic Ocean and Spain, Portugal is a small, vibrant country with a population of over 10 million people. Dancing and singing are massive parts of Portuguese heritage, so in just about every Portuguese village you can find a dance floor (called a ***terreiro***), where you'll see folk music and folk dancing from the region accompanied by guitars, accordions, and even bagpipes!

IBERIAN WOLVES

Iberian wolves, the largest of the wolf population in Western Europe, travel in smaller packs, and even though wolves are predatory animals, they help keep the population of wild boar under control.

Fado music started in the 1820s in cafes in Lisbon. *Fado* means fate, and its lyrics talk about sadness or loss, though some songs include hope for the future.

IBERIAN LYNX

The Iberian lynx have long hair on their feet that helps them move silently over snow (so no crunching) and keeps their bodies warm.

Sitting on Pico Island, **Mount Pico** is the highest mountain in Portugal, standing over 7,000 feet above sea level—and it's a volcano! Though it hasn't erupted since 1720, it is still considered an active volcano.

ATLANTIC OCEAN

Because Portugal's borders extend far into the Atlantic Ocean to include islands like the Azores, about 95% of the country's territory is ocean!

WHOA! Portugal's Luís Filipe was king for only 20 minutes! His reign is tied with King Louis XIX of France's for the shortest reign of a monarch.

Lisbon is home to the world's **oldest bookstore**, Bertrand's Bookstore, which first opened in 1732.

★ **LISBON**

BIRDS

Over 600 species of birds live in Portugal. Not only is the climate warm enough to welcome birds, but it's also the perfect rest stop for birds migrating from Africa.

Las Maravillas Grotto, or the Cave of Wonders, lives up to its name. It has just under a mile and a half of caves decorated with stalactites (mineral formations that hang from the ceiling like icicles) and stalagmites (mineral formations that stick up from the floor). These formations have created underground "rooms," as well as underground lakes.

Riotinto Mining Park is much more than an old mining basin in the Tinto River. Because of its red rocks, river, and little plant life, it reminded NASA and the European Space Agency of Mars. The area is used by both agencies to run experiments for Mars-based exploration!

ANTHONY OF PADUA

LIFESPAN: August 15, 1195–June 13, 1231
BIRTHPLACE: Lisbon, Portugal

Anthony was a Portuguese Roman Catholic priest who was known for his powerful preaching, knowledge of the Bible, and care for the poor and the sick. His teaching helped people who had wandered far from God turn back to Him.

EL CID

LIFESPAN: c. 1043–July 10, 1099
BIRTHPLACE: Vivar, Spain

El Cid is known as the national hero of Spain, fighting for his king, country, and Christianity. There is even an epic poem and a play honoring his heroics.

LEARN THE LANGUAGE

PORTUGUESE

OLÁ (OH-lah): hello

OBRIGADO (OH-bree-GAH-doh): thank you

ADEUS (AH-dee-ohs): goodbye

CASTILIAN SPANISH SLANG

GUAY (gwahee): cool; awesome

NO PASA NADA (NO pah-sah NAH-dah): This phrase literally means "nothing is happening," but it's used like the phrase "no worries" in English.

AMAZING!

You probably don't take a siesta (or nap) after lunch anymore, but sometimes a healthy meal and rest is exactly what you need! In 1 Kings 19, God had called the prophet Elijah to do some really hard things, and he was exhausted, scared, and sad. So what did God do to help him? **While Elijah was sleeping, He sent an angel to give Elijah some bread and water.** After a snack and a nap, Elijah felt better and had the strength to keep serving God.

FRANCE

Each July as part of the **San Fermín Festival**, the city of Pamplona hosts "**the running of the bulls**." Bulls and steers are released into barricaded streets, joined by mozos, or runners, for a short run to a bullring. It's a dangerous tradition, but thousands of people still join in each year.

KEY FACTS

OFFICIAL LANGUAGE:
PORTUGAL: Portuguese
SPAIN: Castilian Spanish

CAPITAL CITY:
PORTUGAL: Lisbon
SPAIN: Madrid

NATIONAL TREE:
PORTUGAL: Cork oak
SPAIN: Holm oak

NATIONAL BIRD:
PORTUGAL: Barcelos rooster
SPAIN: Iberian imperial eagle

If you're up for a food fight, visit the **city of Buñol** to take part in their yearly tomato-throwing festival called La Tomatina!

EURASIAN BEAVERS
The largest rodent in Spain is the Eurasian beaver. These guys can weigh up to 66 pounds!

★ MADRID

SPANISH IBEX
The Spanish ibex have a clever way to help their herds escape danger. When a threat is spotted, the oldest male in the group will lead all the male ibexes to safety, and the oldest female ibex will do the same for the females.

The beautiful basilica (or a big church) **La Sagrada Familia** in Barcelona has been under construction for over 140 years. Construction began in 1882, and it's set to finish in the year 2026, which means it's taking longer to build than it took ancient Egyptians to build the pyramids!

You can walk over 300 feet in the air along a sheer cliff at **Caminito del Rey**. The path is a completely flat, one-way bridge that takes you through the canyons and valleys of the **Desfiladero de los Gaitanes** gorge.

MEDITERRANEAN SEA

SPAIN

EXPLORE THE COUNTRY
With a population of almost 48 million people, Spain is a fascinating country on the Mediterranean Sea filled with beaches, historic castles, and snowy mountains. Its people have a diverse history, with generations of Castilians, Arabs, Jews, Roma, Basques, and Romans making the country what it is today. Like people from many countries in Europe, Spaniards include rest in their days. Though it's not as typical in modern times, it used to be common practice for people to take a quick nap (called a siesta) after lunch each day.

Though the United Kingdom is made up of four countries (England, Wales, Scotland, and Northern Ireland), the island is smaller in size than the US state of Oregon. **No spot in the UK is more than 77 miles from the ocean!**

The tallest mountain in the UK is **Ben Nevis** in Scotland, at 4,412 feet. That would take over 120 buses stacked longways to reach that height!

Scotland has **421 words** to describe snow! You may not get a day off from school if there's a *flindrikin* (a light snow shower), but you would for a blizzard!

WOW!

EUROPEAN HEDGEHOGS
While hedgehogs might be considered an exotic pet in some parts of the world, these little spiky critters are native to the United Kingdom. It's not unusual to see a wild one walking through your garden!

Loch Ness in Scotland is the largest freshwater lake by volume in the UK (and the home of the famed mythical creature the Loch Ness Monster).

SCOTLAND

RED DEER
The largest land mammal in the UK and one of the largest deer in the world is the red deer. These deer have massive antlers that can weigh up to 33 pounds and span over three feet in width!

The Royal Observatory in Edinburgh, Scotland, is not only a massive observatory, but it's also a historical site. The building was finished in 1896 and has been the site of astronomical research and space observation for years.

★ EDINBURGH

ATLANTIC OCEAN

AMAZING

The country of Wales has a town whose name has over 50 letters! The city is called Llanfairpwll-gwyngyllgogerychwyrndrob-wllllantysiliogogogoch, but it also goes by Llanfairpwll (ssshhhANNE-fire-puh-shh), or Llanfair PG for short.

★ BELFAST

NORTHERN IRELAND

DOMESTIC COWS
Domestic cows are considered to be a real danger in the UK because they are so prone to stampeding. Being trampled under a cow stampede or kicked or charged by a cow is a real, deadly threat in the English countryside!

IRELAND

EUROPEAN ADDERS
There is only one kind of venomous snake in the United Kingdom: the European adder.

Ever wanted a card from a real-life king or queen? If you live to be 100, 105, or every birthday after your 105th, you'll get a birthday card from the king himself!

Completed in 2012, The Shard is the **tallest skyscraper** in the United Kingdom. Situated near the iconic Tower Bridge, the Shard is now part of the stunning view of the London skyline.

ENGLAND

WALES

LEARN THE LANGUAGE

★ CARDIFF  ★ LONDON

Stonehenge, a collection of prehistoric rocks stacked in a circle, is one of the oldest monuments in the world. Its origins are still a mystery!

SCOTTISH SLANG

COO (KOO): cow

BONNIE LASS (BON-ee lass): beautiful girl

COORIE (COO-ree): to nestle or cuddle, especially when it is cold outside

ENGLISH CHANNEL

Adventurous swimmers can test their endurance at the **English Channel**, the body of water separating the UK from France. This challenging 21-mile swim is made harder by strong currents, weather changes, and cold temperatures. About 300 people attempt to swim the English Channel each year!

C. S. LEWIS

LIFESPAN: November 29, 1898–November 22, 1963

BIRTHPLACE: Belfast, Northern Ireland

C. S. Lewis was a Christian author known for writing books like the Chronicles of Narnia series. He was also part of a writers' group that included other famous authors like J. R. R. Tolkien, who wrote the Lord of the Rings series!

FRIENDSHIP

J. R. R. Tolkien's strong faith had a big impact on C. S. Lewis becoming a Christian, and Lewis encouraged Tolkien to finish writing and publish The Lord of the Rings. **Good friends support us and draw us closer to God.** Ecclesiastes 4:9–10 tells us, "Two people are better off than one, for they can help each other succeed. If one person falls, the other can reach out and help" (NLT).

SAINT PATRICK

LIFESPAN: c. 401–c. 500

BIRTHPLACE: England

Saint Patrick was a missionary who was known for spreading Christianity throughout Ireland. He is said to have used a three-leaf shamrock to teach about the Trinity—God, Jesus, and the Holy Spirit.

FAITH

When the original concept for The Shard was presented, people were worried that such a large skyscraper would ruin the view of London. However, it is now an iconic part of the city view. In the same way, when Jesus was crucified on the cross, it was not a symbol of faith or Christianity at the time. But because of Jesus' life and resurrection, **the cross has now become the view**—a symbol of Christianity and a reminder of all that Jesus has done for us.

Tennis anyone? Held outside of London, the **Wimbledon Championships** is the oldest and most famous tennis tournament in the world. It began in 1877 and is held for two weeks in England each year. Members of England's royal family have been attending since 1907, and you can spot them in the Royal Box at Centre Court each year.

KEY FACTS

OFFICIAL LANGUAGES: English, Scots Gaelic (Scotland), English Welsh (Wales)

CAPITAL CITY: London

NEIGHBORING COUNTRIES & BODIES OF WATER: Ireland, the English Channel, the North Sea, the Atlantic Ocean

NATIONAL TREE: Oak

NATIONAL BIRD: Robin

NATIONAL DISH: Chicken tikka masala, a chicken dish that is served in a sauce made from tomato, yogurt or cream, and Indian spices

UNITED KINGDOM

EXPLORE THE COUNTRY

The United Kingdom is a commonwealth, or a group of united countries across the globe. Though it has many territories around the world, the United Kingdom (or UK) is an island made up of the countries of England, Scotland, Wales, and Northern Ireland, with over 67 million residents. A major center for Western literature, the UK was home to the likes of poets, playwrights, and authors including William Shakespeare, J. R. R. Tolkien, Chaucer, Jane Austen, and T. S. Eliot. As with most of Europe, you can find ancient castles scattered all across the United Kingdom while also enjoying modern, busy cities like London, Glasgow, and Belfast.

JOHN CALVIN

LIFESPAN: 1509–1564
BIRTHPLACE: Noyon, France

John was a French theologian, pastor, and reformer during the Protestant Reformation.

AMAZING

France is the number-one tourist destination in the entire world, with over 90 million visitors from around the globe stopping by each year!

PALACE OF VERSAILLES

The **Eiffel Tower**, including its broadcast antenna, is 1,083 feet tall.

BELGIUM

PARIS

France is the **largest country in Western Europe**. It is a little smaller than the US state of Texas.

In 2018, over 10 million people visited the iconic art museum called the **Louvre** (LOOV). The museum hosts art from artists around the world, and about 66% of the art displayed came from French artists!

NOTRE DAME CATHEDRAL

GIVE THANKS

France is known for being a country that loves art. Did you know you can use art as a way to express your love and thankfulness to God? It's true! **Colossians 3:17** says, "Whatever you do, whether in word or deed, do it all in the name of the Lord Jesus, giving thanks to God the Father through him" (NIV). The next time you sit down to draw, paint, dance, play music, sing, or craft, remember to pray and thank God for all He's done.

SOUTH GENETS

South genets are incredibly common mammals to spot in the Pyrenees Mountains, especially because of their bushy, striped tails!

On the **Massif Central** plateau, you can find forests, mountains, and some ancient, extinct volcanoes.

France has a pretty **diverse landscape**! You can enjoy warm beaches in the French Riviera, or you can enjoy colder, snowier weather high in the French Alps.

NORTH WOLVES

North wolves used to be extinct in France, but they traveled back from Italy as they lost their habitats in the 1990s. They are still considered to be endangered in France, but now there are almost 200 north wolves living in the French Alps!

ANDORRA

MONACO

The **Tour de France** is the biggest bicycle race in the world, held yearly since 1903. This test of endurance takes place over three weeks. Each day is called a "stage," in which cyclists compete in races with a flat, hilly, or mountainous terrain. The race routes change each year, but the competition always ends at Paris's most famous avenue, the Champs-Élysées.

MEDITERRANEAN SEA

SPAIN

FRANCE

EXPLORE THE COUNTRY — **A country found between the Atlantic Ocean** and the Mediterranean Sea, France is a country with over 66 million people who are known for their love of high fashion, amazing food, expert baking, and breathtaking art. One of the oldest nations in the world, France is home to famous museums like the Louvre; some of the most famous landmarks in the world like the Eiffel Tower, Notre Dame Cathedral, and the Palace at Versailles; and some of the most famous artwork like the *Mona Lisa*.

LEARN THE LANGUAGE

FRENCH

BONJOUR (bohn-JOOR): hello

AU REVOIR (oh REV-wahr): goodbye

JE M'APPELLE (jeh MAH-pell): my name is

ITALIAN

SI (see): yes

GRAZIE (GRAH-tsee-eh): thank you

ITALY

EXPLORE THE COUNTRY Italy is a boot-shaped country that is surrounded by several bodies of water, including the Adriatic Sea, the Mediterranean Sea, and the Tyrrhenian Sea. It has a population of nearly 60 million people and is home to one of the oldest cities in the world, Rome. Italy is home to places like the Colosseum in Rome, a landmark that dates all the way back to biblical times, and Venice, a city built on a waterway that is full of architecture and history from the 1700s and beyond. Italians love good food, and you won't have to travel far in Italy to find some delicious pasta.

KEY FACTS

OFFICIAL LANGUAGE:
FRANCE: French
ITALY: Italian

CAPITAL CITY:
FRANCE: Paris
ITALY: Rome

NATIONAL BIRD:
FRANCE: Gallic rooster
ITALY: Italian sparrow

NATIONAL DISH:
FRANCE: Pot-au-Feu, a dish of stewed meat and veggies
ITALY: Ragu alla bolognese, pasta with a meat-based tomato sauce

---

SWITZERLAND

The highest mountain in Italy is also the highest mountain in the Alps. The mountain is called **Mont Blanc** and is over 15,000 feet above sea level.

Italy is the perfect place to visit if you love water. Not only is the country surrounded by the sea, but there are also over 1,500 lakes.

Gondola rides are a popular tourist attraction in Venice, Italy. A gondola is a thin flat-bottomed boat, and there are about 400 in service today.

The Last Supper by Leonardo da Vinci is one of the most famous pieces of artwork in the world! Located in Santa Maria delle Grazie in Milan, Italy, this masterpiece depicts the final meal Jesus had with His 12 disciples. The painting is over 500 years old, and visitors from all over the world come to view the painting every day.

Construction of the Colosseum ended in AD 80. It originally had 80 arches on each level, but only 31 are still intact on the ground level.

ROME

ADRIATIC SEA

CROATIA

BOSNIA-HERZEGOVINA

MONTENEGRO

The three main active volcanoes in Italy are **Etna, Vesuvius, and Stromboli**. Mount Etna erupted in 2023 and still has steam rising from its peak, Mount Stromboli is currently active, and Mount Vesuvius hasn't erupted since 1944.

The **city of Rome** was founded in 753 BC, but it is in a country that is less than 200 years old. The region underwent a lot of turmoil and border disputes, so the area we know as Italy wasn't officially formed until AD 1861.

MOUNT VESUVIUS

ALBANIA

EUROPEAN HEDGEHOGS
Did you know that even though the European hedgehog is small, they can be covered in up to 7,000 little spines? They use them to protect themselves, curling into a tight ball when they feel scared.

The first four **COSMO-SkyMed satellites** were developed by the Italian Space Agency. These satellites can collect 1,800 images per day as they orbit Earth.

SPECTACLED SALAMANDERS
Italy's spectacled salamander has a unique method to ward off predators. Instead of puffing up its body or rolling into a ball, this lizard simply raises up its tail and legs to show off its bright-red underside to scare away any predators.

GREECE

NETHERLANDS

EXPLORE THE COUNTRY
The Netherlands is found in northwestern Europe, situated between Germany, Belgium, and the North Sea. This country is the home to nearly 18 million people. The Netherlands is famous for their wooden shoes and canals, but there is so much more to this country! You can find more flowers in the Netherlands than anywhere else in the world, and they have regular festivals to celebrate and show off their gorgeous flowers, specifically tulips. The Dutch people also love creating, with their baked goods, cheeses, and paintings known around the world. For instance, painters like Vincent van Gogh and Rembrandt were born in the Netherlands.

SWITZERLAND

UNITED KINGDOM

EXPLORE THE COUNTRY
While the Alps run through several countries in Europe, Switzerland might be the country most commonly associated with the iconic mountain range. The country has a population of just over 8 million people that live between the snowy Alps, crystal-blue alpine lakes, and bright-green grassy valleys. It's a country straight out of a storybook, and the influence of French, German, Italian, and Romansh cultures have created a unique and diverse country. Switzerland puts a high importance on education and is also known for its amazing food, specifically its cheese and super yummy chocolate!

LOVE OTHERS
In John 15:13, Jesus said, **"Greater love has no one than this: to lay down one's life for one's friends"** (NIV). Corrie ten Boom was brave and willing to risk her life to protect others. Likewise, lots of people, like soldiers, police officers, and firefighters, risk their lives each day to protect us. Say a prayer of thanks for these people!

CORRIE TEN BOOM
LIFESPAN: April 15, 1892–April 15, 1983
BIRTHPLACE: Haarlem, Netherlands

Corrie was a strong Christian and the first licensed female watchmaker in Holland. When World War II broke out, she and her family risked their lives to hide Jewish people escaping persecution in a secret room in the family's home.

GERMANY

EXPLORE THE COUNTRY
Germany is a country in the northern central part of Europe, finding itself smack in the middle of the continent. The Alps, one of the major mountain ranges in Europe, crosses through Germany, but the country also has impressive beaches as it borders the Baltic Sea and the North Sea. With over 85 million people, Germany isn't just the home to gorgeous rivers, forests, and mountains, but also medieval castles, stunning folklore, literature, and art. While much of Germany is quite modern, there are some regions in the Black Forest where you will see people wearing traditional clothing known as *tracht* to celebrate holidays.

KEY FACTS

OFFICIAL LANGUAGES:
NETHERLANDS: Dutch and Frisian
SWITZERLAND: French, German, Italian, and Romansh
GERMANY: German

CAPITAL CITY:
NETHERLANDS: Amsterdam
SWITZERLAND: Bern
GERMANY: Berlin

NATIONAL TREE:
NETHERLANDS: Witch
SWITZERLAND: Pinus cembra
GERMANY: Oak

NORWAY

EXPLORE THE COUNTRY

Norway is a country that is found between the Arctic Ocean, Sweden, and Finland on the western portion of the Scandinavian Peninsula. (Scandinavia is the region of Europe that includes Denmark, Norway, and Sweden.) Over half of the country is covered in mountains, but there are also gorgeous beaches and fjords (waterways that reach super far inland) to enjoy when the weather is warmer. Norway is famous for being the home of the Vikings and explorers like Eric the Red. However, the country is also a major hub for fishermen. Norway puts a lot of importance on its folktales of pixies, trolls, and other fairy-tale creatures, and traditional clothing called the **bunad** (a woven wool outfit with colorful accessories) are still worn for festivals today.

Svalbard is a remote group of islands, called an archipelago, that is halfway between mainland Norway and the North Pole. In this Arctic desert you can see arctic animals like polar bears, walruses, and arctic foxes.

You can stay in a **hotel made of ice** in the Swedish village of Jukkasjärvi! Because it's made of ice, the hotel has to be rebuilt each year. They carve the Ice Hotel from a big block of ice they take from the Torne River.

You can see the **northern lights** in Norway from September to April, and places like Lofoten, Bodø, and Tromsø are your best bet to get a good view of the celestial light show.

The **fjords in Norway** are beautiful and full of fish! The water is nutrient-dense, which makes it a happy home to a wide variety of fish, including cod, the most common one to catch!

NORWEGIAN SEA

People living in the northern regions of Sweden get fewer than five hours of sunlight during the winter! To help people get vitamin D, bus stops have **little lightboxes** to simulate sunlight.

WOLVERINES
Don't let a wolverine's small size fool you! These little guys are infamous for their intense strength and their ability to take down prey several times their size.

ARCTIC FOXES
Arctic foxes are either white or blue (bluish gray). Blue arctic foxes stay the same color year-round, but white arctic foxes only have white fur in winter. In the summer, their fur turns gray with dark fur on their legs to blend in with their environment.

Norway has the **longest coastline in Europe** and the second longest in the entire world. It's over 60,000 miles long!

Norway knighted a penguin! **Brigadier Sir Nils Olav III** is both the mascot and colonel-in-chief of the Norwegian King's Guard. And as you might've guessed from his name, he is the third penguin to fill this role!

Over half of **Sweden is covered in forestland**! While much of that is privately owned and not a national park, the Swedish government always plants a new tree after one is cut down to keep the forests healthy.

GULF OF BOTHNIA

OSLO ★   ★ STOCKHOLM

BALTIC SEA

MOOSE
Sweden has the densest population of moose on Earth. In the summer, there are up to 400,000 moose wandering around the forests! However, it's tough to spot them in the wild as, unlike deer, moose travel by themselves and not in herds.

Wild berries grow, well, wildly in Norway. If you're craving a berry or two, you can forage for blueberries, smaller cranberries, and a unique plant that isn't really known outside of Scandinavia called the **yellow cloudberry**.

NORTH SEA

EUROPEAN HARES
Found in central and southern Sweden, the European hare has a unique eye shape that enables it to see 360 degrees around without moving its head. If the hare spots a predator and needs to run, it can reach speeds of up to 50 miles per hour!

Using buildings and statues across the country, Sweden has a **scale model of the solar system** starting in Stockholm and extending nearly 600 miles to the city of Kiruna. One of the largest spherical buildings in the world is the Avicii Arena, also known as the Globe, which serves as the Sun. Statues scattered throughout Sweden model the planets, identified asteroids, dwarf planets, and comets.

DENMARK

GERMANY

SWEDEN

KEY FACTS

OFFICIAL LANGUAGES:
NORWAY: Norwegian and Sami
SWEDEN: Swedish

CAPITAL CITY:
NORWAY: Oslo
SWEDEN: Stockholm

NATIONAL FLOWER:
NORWAY: Pyramidal saxifrage
SWEDEN: Harebell

NATIONAL BIRD:
NORWAY: White-throated dipper
SWEDEN: Eurasian blackbird

EXPLORE THE COUNTRY

Over 10 million people live in Sweden, a country that is nestled between Norway and the Baltic Sea, sharing a northern border with Finland. About 15% of the country is in the Arctic Circle, which means that from late May until the middle of July, this region doesn't see the sun set at all. Known as a country that's committed to caring for creation, Sweden has some of the cleanest air in the world and is a leader in environmental research. This green country is covered in rich forests that are full of mushroom plants and delicious berries like the unique lingonberry.

FREDRIK OLAUS NILSSON

LIFESPAN: July 28, 1809–October 21, 1881
BIRTHPLACE: Varö, Sweden

Fredrik Olaus, known as F. O., was a devout Christian, pastor, and missionary, and he was a vital part in bringing religious freedom to Sweden.

COME TO ME

Rest is important to the Swedes, but the Bible also talks about the importance of rest. Matthew 11:28 says, **"Come to me, all you who are weary and burdened, and I will give you rest"** (NIV). When we are feeling overwhelmed, the best place to go for rest is Jesus. The next time you are feeling worried, take a few deep breaths and spend some time in prayer telling God what is on your mind and giving your burdens to Him!

AMAZING

Swedes observe something called *fika*, which is an official break from work that typically includes coffee and a snack like *kanelbullar*—cinnamon buns! Companies are expected to make sure their employees take these breaks. It makes sense why Sweden is always in the top five happiest countries in the world!

ANNIE SKAU BERNTSEN

LIFESPAN: May 29, 1911– November 26, 1992
BIRTHPLACE: Oslo, Norway

Annie was a nurse and missionary who served in China until missionaries were forced to leave the country in 1951. She continued helping Chinese refugees until she retired.

LEARN THE LANGUAGE

NORWEGIAN

EVENTYRLYSTEN (EH-vent-teer-lee-sten): the desire to explore new places

FRILUFTSLIV (FREE-lufts-liv): the love of spending time in nature

SWEDISH

GOD DAG (GOO dah): good day

HEJSAN (HEY-san): hello

KEY FACTS

OFFICIAL LANGUAGE:
CZECHIA: Czech
POLAND: Polish

CAPITAL CITY:
CZECHIA: Prague
POLAND: Warsaw

NATIONAL TREE:
CZECHIA: Small-leaved lime
POLAND: Oak

NATIONAL BIRD:
CZECHIA: Moravian eagle
POLAND: White-tailed eagle

EUROPEAN BISON
The European bison, also known as the wisent, is the heaviest land animal in Europe. These animals are often found in the forests of Poland and can weigh more than 1,322 pounds. That's heavier than a grand piano!

In the 1500s, Polish astronomer **Nicolaus Copernicus** was the first person to theorize that the planets revolve around the Sun. Before this, people believed that the Sun and the stars revolved around Earth.

Near the town of Gryfino is a peculiar, mysterious forest called **Krzywy Las, the Crooked Forest**. About 400 pine trees bend in identical J shapes, curving in the same direction, but no one knows why! Some speculate that the area has a unique gravitational pull or that heavy snowfall weighed down the trees when they were young; others think the trees were bent by foresters who wanted curved wood for building furniture.

AGNES OF BOHEMIA
LIFESPAN: January 20, 1211– March 2, 1282
BIRTHPLACE: Bohemia

Agnes was a princess, but instead of living a life of royal luxury, she devoted herself to her faith, charity, and helping others.

Prague Castle holds the Guinness World Record for being the largest ancient castle in the world!

Czechia has the most castles of any country in Europe, housing over 2,000!

Mount Snezka is the tallest mountain in Czechia at 5,259 feet tall.

PRAGUE
The capital **city of Prague** has been considered the most beautiful city in Europe since the 18th century.

The **largest telescope** in Czechia, Perek's 2-m telescope, weighs over 80 tons and is over 50 years old. But it's still in great shape and has been in operation at the **Astronomical Institute at the Czech Academy of Sciences** in Ondřejov since 1967!

Czechia's Hranice Abyss is the deepest freshwater cave in the world, but the exact depth is unknown. Divers reached 1,325 feet underwater, but their equipment wouldn't allow them to go deeper. New research shows that the abyss is likely over 3,280 feet deep—or more!

CESKY TERRIERS
The Cesky terrier is a dog from Czechia that is great at hunting prey and sniffing out underground fox dens.

CZECHIA

EXPLORE THE COUNTRY
The Czech Republic, or Czechia, is surrounded by Poland, Germany, Slovakia, and Austria with a population of over 10 million people. This country is so beautiful that Shakespeare took notice and set his play *A Winter's Tale* there. Czechia is over 1,000 years old and has thousands of gorgeous castles. One of the most famous is called Karlštejn Castle. In Czechia you can find miles of cheerful, bright-yellow canola fields, the ancient Bohemian Forest, and even some mountains.

POLAND

RUSSIA • LITHUANIA • BELARUS • UKRAINE • SLOVAKIA • HUNGARY

EXPLORE THE COUNTRY

Poland is on the shore of the Baltic Sea and is surrounded by countries like Germany, Ukraine, and Belarus. Over 37 million people live in Poland, and the country's history goes back all the way to the 1500s. Poland is full of pretty canola fields, gorgeous rivers, and incredible forests, with beautiful animals throughout its land. And in World War II after their capital city of Warsaw was destroyed, the Polish people banded together and restored the city to its former glory.

Less than 50 copies exist of the original Gutenberg Bible that was made in the 15th century, and you can find one of them in the Diocesan Museum in the Polish town of Pelplin. It was the first notable book to be printed with a printing press.

★ WARSAW

Poland has the only desert in Central Europe. It's called **Pustynia Błędowska**, and it was created thanks to a melting glacier many, many years ago. It's truly a unique sight as the sandy oasis sits right in the middle of lush Polish forests.

Foraging for mushrooms is a favorite pastime for Polish people. They are taught from a young age to tell the difference between edible and poisonous mushrooms.

WHITE STORKS

Each spring, roughly 25% of white storks in the world migrate to Poland. People encourage storks to nest there by building platforms on roofs as well as pole towers. In the small town of Żywkowo, known as the stork capital, you can find more storks than people during the summer!

All Polish names are tied to a particular date on the calendar. Every day on the Polish calendar has a specific male and female name attached to it, just like holidays. Polish people celebrate these days, called Name Days, like birthdays, and it's not unusual for you to get gifts on your Name Day.

SAINT JOHN PAUL II

LIFESPAN: May 18, 1920– April 2, 2005

BIRTHPLACE: Wadowice, Poland

John Paul II was the Pope, the head of the Catholic Church, and sovereign of the Vatican City State from 1978 until his death in 2005. He traveled more than all the previous popes combined because he wanted to encourage people of faith around the world.

AMAZING!

If we've learned anything from the grandness of Hranice Abyss, it's that we've still not seen all the wonders of God's creation. Psalm 139:14 says **God's workmanship, or creation, is marvelous**—there are lots of new things to discover each day!

You can explore **Wieliczka Salt Mine**, an 800-year-old salt mine that has not only been producing salt since the 13th century, but it also has a massive cathedral carved out from rock salt within the mines!

LEARN THE LANGUAGE

CZECH

PROSÍM (pro-SEEM): please

DĚKUJI VÁM (dye-KOO-yi vam): thank you

POLISH

NA ZDROWIE (nas-DRO-v-yea): cheers

DZIEŃ DOBRY (jine-dobree): good day

PROSZĘ (proshe): please

65

SLOVAKIA

CZECHIA

There are **9 national parks and 14 protected landscape areas** in Slovakia. From the tall peaks found in the High Tatras where you can hike or ski in the winter to the caves in Slovak Paradise, there's a lot of creation to explore!

EXPLORE THE COUNTRY
Slovakia is a smaller country with over 5 million residents, but it's small size doesn't mean it's short on beauty. Slovakia has lots of snow-capped mountains and gorgeous bodies of water. The Danube River flows through Slovakia, and there are several gorgeous lakes such as Štrbské Pleso in the High Tatra Mountains. Slovakians are also serious about celebrating! Christmas celebrations last three days, and Easter is one of the biggest celebrations of the year.

There are over **6,000 caves** in Slovakia!

One style of folk dance comes from the Orava region of Slovakia. Their dance called **Cepovy** is a high-energy dance that is meant to represent the way Slovakians used to harvest grains.

★ BRATISLAVA

AUSTRIA

PEREGRINE FALCONS
The fastest recorded speed of a peregrine falcon is 242 miles per hour! It's the fastest bird in the world!

★ BUDAPEST

EURASIAN LYNX
The Eurasian lynx is found all over Europe and Asia, but it tends to stick to the higher altitude forests of Slovakia. You'll mostly find these protected cats in Slovakian national parks.

Budapest is known as the **"city of baths"** because it has more hot springs than any other capital city in the world. The thermal waters, which stay warm year-round, contain trace minerals that are said to have health benefits, including healing some skin conditions.

Lake Balaton is the largest lake in Central Europe. It's a freshwater lake along the Bakony Mountains that is 48 miles long, and the deepest point of the lake goes down 37 feet.

LEARN THE LANGUAGE

SLOVAK
- **DOBRÝ DEŇ** (DOH-bree denya): hello
- **DOBRÉ RÁNO** (DOH-brehh RAA-noh): good morning
- **DOBRÚ NOC** (DOH-broo nohts): good night

HUNGARIAN
- **SZIA** (seeya): hello

ROMANIAN
- **SALUT** (SAH-loo): hello
- **CIAO** (chow): bye

ELIZABETH OF HUNGARY
LIFESPAN: July 7, 1207–November 17, 1231
BIRTHPLACE: Pressburg, Hungary

Elizabeth was a princess and married at a young age. When her husband died, she received a large sum of money, and instead of using the money for herself, she opened a hospital and worked there to help care for the sick.

HUNGARY

EXPLORE THE COUNTRY
Hungary is a landlocked country surrounded by countries like Romania and Ukraine and has over 9 million people living there. Most citizens of Hungary, called Magyarország by Hungarians, live in the capital city of Budapest. Hungarians are incredibly passionate about theater, opera, and literature, and they tend to use art as a way to express their feelings and discuss their own history and folklore.

POLAND

RICHARD WURMBRAND

LIFESPAN: March 24, 1909– February 17, 2001

BIRTHPLACE: Bucharest, Romania

Richard was a pastor who was arrested in Communist Romania for preaching about Jesus and speaking out against Communism. He spent years in prison, but he never abandoned his faith. Years after his release, he and his wife cofounded a ministry to help families of Christians imprisoned for their faith.

The Romanian Space Agency built a microsatellite called the ROM-2 that is about the size of a Rubik's Cube but can take high resolution photos of Earth when in orbit. It's the first of its kind, and the satellite's small size will drastically lower the cost of sending a satellite to space.

FAITH

The ROM-2 may be a tiny satellite, but it can do quite a lot. Matthew 17:20–21 tells us that if we have faith the size of a tiny mustard seed, we can move mountains. **In God's eyes, even small things can have a great impact for the kingdom of God.**

KEY FACTS

OFFICIAL LANGUAGE:
SLOVAKIA: Slovak
HUNGARY: Hungarian
ROMANIA: Romanian

CAPITAL CITY:
SLOVAKIA: Bratislava
HUNGARY: Budapest
ROMANIA: Bucharest

NATIONAL TREE:
SLOVAKIA: Linden
HUNGARY: Acacia
ROMANIA: Oak

NATIONAL BIRD:
SLOVAKIA: Golden eagle
HUNGARY: Turul
ROMANIA: Golden eagle

EUROPEAN BADGERS

The European badger might technically be a carnivore (meaning they eat only meat), but they're not picky eaters. They're known for chowing down on worms and slugs!

The Transfagarasan Highway is famous for its beauty and a unique driving experience. It runs through the mountain passes of the Southern Carpathians, and the road itself is full of twists, turns, and tunnels that let you test your driving skills while taking in gorgeous views.

BROWN BEARS

If you want to see a brown bear, your chances are pretty high in Romania, as the country is home to the largest population of brown bears in all of Europe.

On the Danube River you can see not only some incredible nature but also a really cool sculpture carved into the rock of the **Iron Gates Gorge**. It's the face of Decebalus, an ancient king who fought against the Roman Empire.

WILD HORSES

The Danube Delta is an old nature preserve where you can encounter massive amounts of wild horses. They are some of the last groups of wild horses in Europe, and there are estimated to be over 5,000 of them in the area!

★ BUCHAREST

BLACK SEA

ROMANIA

BULGARIA

SERBIA

EXPLORE THE COUNTRY — **A country on the Black Sea, Romania is divided pretty evenly among mountain ranges,** hills, and forests. Over 18 million people live in the country. Romanians celebrate Christian holidays like Christmas and Easter in big ways, even breaking out some traditional clothing to mark the occasion. While each Romanian community has their own unique traditional clothes, they all usually wear outfits that are heavily embroidered and made of silk.

The nightingale is a special bird to Ukrainians, and the sounds of its cheerful chirping are seen as signs that peace and happiness are returning after winter. **Ukrainians view nightingales as the symbol of new beginnings.**

VLADIMIR THE GREAT

LIFESPAN: c. 956–July 15, 1015
BIRTHPLACE: Kyiv, Ukraine

Vladimir was the grand prince of Kyiv and was the first Christian ruler in the region. He built churches and increased the reach of Christianity in the nation while also using his power to help those in need, increasing aid to the poor and expanding educational institutions.

SAIGA ANTELOPE

The saiga antelope are easy to spot thanks to their wide nose. But their nose isn't just for looks! It helps filter dust, as these antelopes tend to live in drier, dustier locations. It also helps heat the air when the weather gets cold, so their mating calls sound louder! And because of the low population of these antelope, conservationists are helping to increase their number in Ukraine.

KEY FACTS

OFFICIAL LANGUAGE: Ukrainian

CAPITAL CITY: Kyiv

NEIGHBORING COUNTRIES & BODIES OF WATER: Russia, Belarus, Poland, Slovakia, Hungary, Romania, Moldova, Black Sea, Sea of Azov

NATIONAL TREE: Viburnum willow

NATIONAL BIRD: None

NATIONAL DISH: Borscht, a soup made of red beets

DOING GOOD

Ukraine is one of the most **fertile** places on earth, which makes this country an ideal place to plant and produce crops. After months and even years of growing, watering, and taking care of seeds, harvesters are able to see the results of their time and effort as they collect their harvest. Just like the harvesters, we can be diligent in taking good care of the things that God has given us! **Galatians 6:9** says, "Let us not become weary in doing good, for at the proper time we will reap a harvest if we do not give up" (NIV).

RUSSIA

Ukraine has the ideal conditions for growing **wheat crops**! In fact, the country is sometimes called the "breadbasket of Europe" because the country produces so much wheat.

Ukraine's national flower is the **sunflower**, and for good reason! The country is the largest producer of sunflower seeds in the entire world. In fact, if you dug up all the sunflowers in Ukraine, you could cover the entire country of Slovenia with them!

SEA OF AZOV

UKRAINE

EXPLORE THE COUNTRY

Ukraine is a country that is nestled between Russia and the Black Sea and has a population of over 43 million people. Ukraine only gained its independence in 1991, but it's a country full of culture and life. Folk music and folk dancing are still incredibly important today, and groups like the Verovka State Chorus and the Virsky Dance Ensemble keep those arts alive by bringing them to the stage across the country. Only five percent of Ukraine is made up of mountains, and the rest of the country is filled with plains, hills, rivers, and gorges.

LEARN THE LANGUAGE

RUSSIAN

ДА (da): yes

НЕТ (nyet): no

ПОЖАЛУЙСТА (po-ZHA-lus-ta): please

СПАСИБО (spa-SI-buh): thank you

SERAPHIM OF SAROV

LIFESPAN: July 19, 1759–January 2, 1833
BIRTHPLACE: Kursk, Russia

Seraphim of Sarov is considered to be a saint in the Russian Orthodox church. He spent a lot of his life telling people how to have a relationship with God and ways to serve God in everyday life, when at the time that was thought to be something only a priest could experience.

Russia is the **largest country** in the world, making up 11% of the landmass on the entire globe. The country covers 6,601,665 square miles, about twice the size of the second-largest country, Canada, which covers 3,885,101 square miles.

ARCTIC OCEAN

Cathedral of St. Basil the Blessed was commissioned by Ivan the Terrible and built between 1554–1560.

REINDEER

There aren't many animals running around Russia because of its harsh, cold climate. However, large animals like reindeer (also called caribou) are able to survive and thrive through the harsh winters. It is believed that there are about a million reindeer living in Russia.

Russia is home to Europe's largest building, the **Lakhta Center**, which is 87 stories tall!

Around 20% of all the Earth's trees are found in Russia. That's about **640 billion trees!**

★ **MOSCOW**

The longest river in Europe, the **Volga River**, is found in Russia. It is over 2,000 miles long!

FAITH

About 71% of Russians identify as Orthodox Christian, 15% don't identify with any religion, and 5% are Muslim.

In 1961, the Soviet Union sent the first person to space, Yuri Gagarin. Gagarin spent just under two hours in space aboard the spacecraft **Vostok 1** and successfully made it back to Earth after completing an entire orbit around the planet.

The highest peak in Europe is found in the **Caucasus Mountains** in Russia. Mount Elbrus is 18,510 feet above sea level!

BLACK SEA

KAZAKHSTAN

CASPIAN SEA

RUSSIA

EXPLORE THE COUNTRY

Russia has a population of over 144 million people and is the world's largest country. Because the country is so large, it has 11 different time zones! Russia has the world's lowest recorded temperatures (outside of the North and South Poles), but the country isn't just a big block of ice. Russia is home to some truly amazing forests, as well as gorgeous rivers and lakes. There are over 120 different ethnic groups living in Russia, and many different languages spoken in Russian communities. The country is also known for its contributions in literature, music composition, and ballet.

Oymyakon, Russia, is the coldest village in the entire world. Its average temperature in winter is -58 degrees Fahrenheit, but the coldest recorded temperature got all the way down to -96 degrees Fahrenheit! That's cold enough to make your glasses freeze right to your face just by stepping outside!

TUFTED PUFFINS
The tufted puffin is a bird with shorter wings, so they don't spend as much time in the air as you might expect. They are actually built better for diving and swimming through the water, where they hunt for their prey.

Russia is a transcontinental country. That means it lies in more than one continent: Europe and Asia!

PACIFIC OCEAN

Siberia is a region in Russia that takes up 77% of the country. However, because the conditions are so harsh in the winter, only 20% of Russians live there.

The **Kamchatka Peninsula** holds one of the biggest concentrations of active volcanoes on the planet! One of those volcanoes, Shiveluch, erupted on April 11, 2023, spewing ash over 12 miles high!

SIBERIAN TIGERS
Siberian tigers are one of the world's largest cats, and they have thick fur to keep them warm during the winters. Just like no two humans have the same fingerprints, no two tigers have the same pattern of stripes on their bodies.

AMUR LEOPARDS
The Amur leopard can reach speeds of 37 miles per hour. It is also an expert jumper, able to leap more than 19 feet horizontally and over 10 feet vertically.

COOL!

Matryoshka dolls, or nesting dolls, are popular souvenirs in Russia. These colorful wooden dolls open to reveal another smaller doll, which opens to reveal another smaller doll, and so forth. These toys were first made in 1892.

KEY FACTS

OFFICIAL LANGUAGE: Russian

CAPITAL CITY: Moscow

NEIGHBORING COUNTRIES: Norway, Finland, Estonia, Latvia, Lithuania, Poland, Belarus, Ukraine, Georgia, Azerbaijan, Kazakhstan, China, Mongolia, North Korea, Japan

NATIONAL FLOWER: Chamomile

NATIONAL TREE: Siberian larch

NATIONAL DISH: Pelmeni, a meat dumpling

*The map shows the European portion of Russia only.

GOD HAS A PLAN
Russia is famous for how cold it gets in the winter, but in the summertime, the climate can be lovely. It's important to remember that hardship, like a cold season, doesn't last forever. **Ecclesiastes 3:1** reminds us, "There is a time for everything, and a season for every activity under the heavens" (NIV). God always has a plan, even when the hard times come, and those hard times won't last forever.

CHINA MONGOLIA

BULGARIA

GREECE

BLACK SEA

This northwestern portion of Türkiye is in Europe.

The **Galata Bridge** in Istanbul connects the European and Asian portions of Türkiye. You can easily walk from one continent to the other—it's only about a third of a mile long!

No Turkish astronaut has been to space—at least not yet! In 2021, the Turkish government established Türkiye's National Space Program, with a 10-year goal to send a Turkish astronaut to the International Space Station, land on the Moon, and establish satellite systems.

FUN FACT

One of the biggest and oldest covered markets is in Istanbul. The **Grand Bazaar**, or Kapalı Çarsı, opened for business back in 1455 and houses over 4,000 stores and stretches for 61 streets!

The Netherlands in Europe might be known for its tulips, but it has Türkiye to thank for them! In the 16th century, a Dutch ambassador brought back tulip bulbs from Türkiye. Each April the **Istanbul Tulip Festival honors its national flower**, and the celebration lasts the entire month.

 ANKARA

WHEREVER WE ARE

Istanbul is one of the few cities in the world to be in two continents. So if you stand in just the right place, you could technically be in Europe and Asia at the same time. But did you know the Bible says God is able to be everywhere all at once? **Psalm 139:7-10 says that wherever we are, God is also there.** So even in those moments when you might feel lonely, remember that God is right there with you.

KEY FACTS

OFFICIAL LANGUAGE: Turkish

CAPITAL CITY: Ankara

NEIGHBORING COUNTRIES & BODIES OF WATER: Black Sea, Mediterranean Sea, Georgia, Armenia, Azerbaijan, Iran, Iraq, Syria, Greece, Bulgaria

NATIONAL TREE: Türkiye oak

NATIONAL BIRD: Redwing

NATIONAL DISH: Döner kebab, lamb (or other meats) cooked rotisserie-style and served in a pita or flatbread

CHEVROTAINS
The chevrotain, or mouse deer, is a small hoofed mammal with a pretty impressive way to escape predators. When attacked, they'll leap into the nearest river or stream to hide, staying submerged for up to four minutes!

APOSTLE PAUL
LIFESPAN: c. 4 BC–AD 62
BIRTHPLACE: Tarsus (modern-day Türkiye)

Paul was an incredibly important missionary and evangelist in the early church. After Jesus changed his life, Paul traveled wherever he could preach the gospel, and he wrote much of the New Testament.

CYPRUS

MEDITERRANEAN SEA

TÜRKIYE

LEARN THE LANGUAGE

TURKISH

GÜNAYDIN (goo-nEYE-dun): good morning

NASILSIN? (NAH-sil-sin): How are you?

TEŞEKKÜRLER (teh-sheh-kull-erh): thank you

Türkiye's national sport is **oil wrestling**—yes, wrestling while covered in slippery olive oil!

You can visit **underground cities and caves** in the region of Cappadocia. These cities and caves were used by early Christians fleeing persecution in Rome.

AVOCET BIRDS

Avocet birds have a unique bill that curves upward at the tip. When they search for food in shallow water, they use their bill to stir up dirt and sand to find and filter out the food.

HOW HIGH?

Have you ever wondered how high were the flood waters that covered the Earth in Genesis 6-9? The Bible says in Genesis 8:4 that **Noah's ark came to rest on Mount Ararat**, the tallest point in Türkiye, as the flood waters began to dry up.

Mount Ararat is Türkiye's highest mountain, measuring 16,945 feet above sea level.

One of the oldest Christian church buildings, the **Grotto of St. Peter**, is in Antakya, known as Antioch in the Bible. The church is believed to have been started by Jesus' disciple Simon Peter.

TURKISH VAN CATS

Typically, pet cats do everything they can to avoid getting into water. But the Turkish Van cat loves water! They are known as "swimming cats" and get their name because they are frequently spotted swimming around Türkiye's Lake Van.

Türkiye has almost **13,000 named mountains**, like Mount Aydos at 11,414 feet tall, Uludoruk Peak at 15,563 feet tall, and Demirkazık Peak at 12,320 feet tall.

IRAQ

SYRIA

EXPLORE THE COUNTRY

Türkiye, also known as Turkey, is a country surrounded by the Black Sea and the Mediterranean Sea with a population of over 86 million people. It's bigger than any European country, except Russia. While Türkiye is mostly found in Asia, a small portion of the country near Bulgaria, known as the Turkish Thrace, is considered part of Europe. Türkiye has a lot of mountains and beaches, and while it has some warm summers, the winters are known to get pretty chilly too.

LEBANON

KEY FACTS

OFFICIAL LANGUAGES: Hebrew and Arabic

CAPITAL CITY: Jerusalem

NEIGHBORING COUNTRIES, REGIONS & BODIES OF WATER: Palestine, Lebanon, Syria, Jordan, Egypt, Mediterranean Sea, Dead Sea, Gulf of Aqaba

NATIONAL TREE: Olive Tree

NATIONAL BIRD: Hoopoe

NATIONAL DISH: Falafel (chickpea fritters)

MARY, MOTHER OF JESUS

LIFESPAN: c. 25 BC–c. AD 75
BIRTHPLACE: Nazareth, Israel

God chose Mary to be Jesus' earthly mom, fulfilling many Old Testament prophecies. In Luke 1, when an angel told Mary she would give birth to Jesus, she responded with humility and obedience, saying: "I am the servant girl of the Lord. Let this happen to me as you say!" (v. 38 ICB).

JESUS

EARTHLY LIFESPAN: c. 4 BC–c. AD 30 (but He rose from the dead!)
BIRTHPLACE: Bethlehem, Israel

Jesus is the Son of God. He came to Earth, born as a baby, to fulfill God's plans, which were made before the beginning of the world. He knew that our sin separated us from God, and we couldn't make our way back to Him on our own. So Jesus lived a perfect life and willingly took on our sins as His own. He was killed on a cross and buried in a tomb. But then He rose from the dead, defeating the darkness once and for all so that everyone who believes in Him will experience new life, both now and in eternity to come.

MEDITERRANEAN SEA

WHAT IS FAITH?

God promised Abram in Genesis 15:12–16 that though he wouldn't see the promised land (Israel), his descendants would. Abram, whose name was changed to Abraham, had faith that God would fulfill His promise. What is faith? Hebrews 11:1 tells us, **"Faith is confidence in what we hope for and assurance about what we do not see"** (NIV). Spend some time in prayer today asking God to help you trust Him in faith.

ISRAEL

EXPLORE THE COUNTRY — Israel is a country with just over 9 million people that is surrounded by the Mediterranean Sea and countries like Lebanon and Jordan. The landscape consists of desert to the south, coastal plains and highlands to the north, and a massive valley running through the country. Israel is considered the Holy Land, or the promised land, to the Jewish people and Christians alike. Many events from the Bible occurred in Israel, including the birth of Jesus! And many ancient biblical artifacts, like the Dead Sea Scrolls, have been found there.

LEARN THE LANGUAGE

HEBREW

SHALOM (SHA-loam): hello; goodbye; peace

BOKER TOV (BOW-ker toav): good morning

TODAH (TOE-dah): thank you

PRAYERS

About a million people each year go to Jerusalem to stick notes with prayers into the cracks of the Western Wall, the last remaining stretch of wall that surrounded the Jewish Temple in the Old Testament. You can also mail a prayer to be placed in the wall. Israel's postal service even has a special department for those letters to God.

AMAZING!

The Western Wall is an important historical place where people from all around the world go to visit and pray. But you don't have to go all the way to Israel to talk to God! Ephesians 6:18 says you can "pray in the Spirit on all occasions with all kinds of prayers" and "keep on praying for all the Lord's people" (NIV). So even if you're just sitting in your room, God is ready to talk with you.

LEBANON

SYRIAN HAMSTERS

At the Hebrew University of Jerusalem in 1930, a zoologist domesticated Syrian hamsters so they could become pets. These are now the most common hamsters in the world.

Israel has no shortage of beaches! There are **137 beaches** to enjoy in the country.

SYRIA

Where did Jesus walk on water, calm a storm during a boat ride, and feed the 5,000? Near the **Sea of Galilee** (now Lake Tiberias), a freshwater lake in northern Israel.

LAKE TIBERIAS

Jesus regularly visited the Mount of Olives in Jerusalem. You can read more about this place where He often went to find refuge and pray (Luke 21:37; Luke 22:39) throughout the Gospels.

JORDAN

 JERUSALEM

This is the location of Bethlehem, where Jesus was born.

The **Dead Sea's water is 10 times saltier than the ocean**, which makes it denser and heavier. Because of this, floating in the water takes no effort—it literally pushes people to the surface and won't let them sink.

DEAD SEA

Despite its name, the **Dead Sea** is a lake. It is the lowest point in all of Asia, and because this lake is so incredibly salty, it contains no plant or animal life.

SAND CATS

Sand cats live only in the desert. The thick fur on their paws helps them to walk on hot sand. And though they may look cuddly, sand cats are ferocious predators that will kill venomous snakes.

One of the oldest trees in Israel is a fruit tree called a **jujube tree**, and it's believed to be 1,500 to 2,000 years old.

EGYPT

BEES

Bees are super important because they pollinate the crops we eat, but their numbers are quickly dwindling. Israelis are doing a lot of work to protect the bee population. They developed an autonomous beehive where bees are protected and beekeepers can monitor and care for them through an app on a smartphone.

ARABIAN ORYX

In the 1970s, the Arabian oryx, a species of desert antelope, was considered to be extinct in the wild (only existing in places like zoos). However, thanks to conservation and repopulation efforts, the status of the Arabian oryx moved from extinct to vulnerable in 2011. They were reintroduced into the wild in several countries, including Israel.

129°F

The hottest temperature recorded in Israel was in 1942 in Beit She'an Valley, just west of the Jordan River, at around **129 degrees Fahrenheit**. That's just a bit cooler than the hottest temperature ever recorded (134 degrees Fahrenheit in Death Valley, California, in 1913).

In 2026, NASA will help launch **Israel's first space telescope**, sending the ULTRASAT (Ultraviolet Transient Astronomy Satellite) into space. ULTRASAT is an ultraviolet observatory that will be able to monitor and learn about things happening in space, like supernova explosions and neutron stars merging.

77

KEY FACTS

OFFICIAL LANGUAGE:
JORDAN: Arabic
SAUDI ARABIA: Arabic

CAPITAL CITY:
JORDAN: Amman
SAUDI ARABIA: Riyadh

NATIONAL TREE:
JORDAN: Oak
SAUDI ARABIA: Phoenix palm

NATIONAL FLOWER:
JORDAN: Black iris
SAUDI ARABIA: Arfaj

NATIONAL BIRD:
JORDAN: Sinai rosefinch
SAUDI ARABIA: Falcon

AWESOME!
Al-Maghtas is believed to be the location of the Jordan River where John the Baptist baptized Jesus, and you can visit the spot today! You can also read about Jesus' baptism in Matthew 3:13–17, Mark 1:9–11, Luke 3:21–22, and John 1:29–34.

Jordan has one of the **smallest forested areas** on the planet, with less than 2% of its land being forests. About 15% of the land in most countries is forest.

The desert valley **Wadi Rum** in Jordan is a great place for stargazing because there isn't a lot of light pollution. You can easily spot the Milky Way from there!

The city of Petra is one of the oldest in the world. It's carved out of stone, and its pinkish color makes it a breathtaking sight. But for something so old, only a small portion of it—about 15%—has been explored!

GRIFFON VULTURES
You can find the Griffon vulture in the cliffs of the Asir Mountains. These birds have a terrible sense of smell but amazing sight. They can spot an animal carcass from up to four miles away!

According to Jordanian tradition, it's okay to say no to an **invitation for a meal** up to three times before you are expected to accept.

The King Fahd's Fountain is the world's tallest at over 1,000 feet high. The fountain sprays water at speeds of over 200 miles per hour!

JORDAN

EXPLORE THE COUNTRY **Jordan is a country with just under 11.5 million people** and the site of ancient kingdoms found in the Bible, like Moab, Gilead, and Edom. Despite its ancient roots, Jordan has only been an independent country since 1946. It's a small country, and a motivated hiker can cross the 400 miles it will take to get from one side of the country to the other in 40 days.

SAUDI ARABIA

EXPLORE THE COUNTRY **Saudi Arabia is home to over 32 million people,** and it's a mix of older, traditional ways of life and fast-paced, modern life. Saudi Arabia is home to two major religious sites for people who practice the Islamic faith, so the rules of Islam play a big part in Saudi Arabian society. Though Saudi Arabia is on the coast of the Red Sea, most of the country is desert with a few mountains and plateaus.

IRAQ

HONEY BADGERS
Honey badgers are adorable but ferocious! They digest every part of their prey—including the bones, hair, and feathers!

TALK ABOUT IT
Saudi Arabia only allows people to follow the religion of Islam, but there are still Christians there! **It's dangerous to be a Christian in a place where it's against the law, but the Bible tells us to continue to talk about our love of Jesus, even if we might get into trouble.** First Peter 4:14-16 even says people who do this are blessed!

ELIJAH THE PROPHET
LIFESPAN: c. 900 BC–801 BC
BIRTHPLACE: Tishbe, Jordan

Elijah was a major prophet in the Old Testament, and through God's power he once parted the Jordan River so he and the prophet Elisha could cross it! You can read about it in 2 Kings 2.

SAINT ARETHAS
LIFESPAN: Unknown–AD 523
BIRTHPLACE: Najran, Saudi Arabia

Arethas was the leader of a Christian church in Najran in the 6th century. When Christians were being persecuted for their faith by the Jewish king Dhu Nuwas, Arethas was killed.

KUWAIT

BAHRAIN

PERSIAN GULF

QATAR

IRAN

UNITED ARAB EMIRATES

★ RIYADH

Saudi Arabia doesn't have any rivers! The country is covered in desert, so most of its fresh water comes from underground reservoirs or water plants that remove salt from ocean water.

The largest uninterrupted area of sand is Saudi Arabia's Rub' al-Khali, which means "empty quarter." This area covers over 250,000 square miles. That's bigger than the entire country of Thailand!

Rayyanah Barnawi was the first female Saudi Arabian astronaut to be sent into space. In 2023, she was part of a 10-day mission to the International Space Station.

LEARN THE LANGUAGE

ARABIC TERM USED IN JORDAN

SARAHA (SARE-ah-ha): honestly

ARABIC SLANG USED IN SAUDI ARABIA

YALLAH (YAH-lah): let's go

AKEED (AH-keed): sure; yes, of course

OMAN

ARABIAN WOLVES
Unlike most wolves, Arabian wolves don't travel in packs. Instead, they either hunt on their own, or they travel with just two or three other wolves.

KAZAKHSTAN

Iran doesn't follow the Gregorian calendar like most countries do. **It follows a solar calendar that begins on the first day of spring and ends on the last day of winter.** Another difference? Thursdays and Fridays are considered the weekend instead of Saturdays and Sundays.

TURKMENISTAN

UZBEKISTAN

CASPIAN COBRAS
Caspian cobras have ribs that expand to give them their iconic cobra hood. And that hood isn't an empty threat! The Caspian is one of the most venomous cobras in the world.

TAJIKISTAN

ESTHER

LIFESPAN: Unknown
BIRTHPLACE: Persia (modern-day Iran)

Esther's story can be found in the Old Testament book named after her. She was a Jewish woman who became the queen of Persia. At a time when there was a plot to kill the Jewish people living in Persia, Esther's faith and bravery helped her to save her people.

AFGHANISTAN

ASIATIC BLACK BEARS
Asiatic black bears in Iran spend most of their life in the trees, using their strong limbs and claws to climb. They sometimes make treetop nests to relax in!

KEY FACTS

OFFICIAL LANGUAGE: Farsi

CAPITAL CITY: Tehrān

NEIGHBORING COUNTRIES & BODIES OF WATER: Turkmenistan, Afghanistan, Pakistan, Gulf of Oman, Persian Gulf, Iraq, Türkiye, Armenia, Azerbaijan, Caspian Sea

NATIONAL TREE: Mediterranean cypress

NATIONAL BIRD: Common nightingale

NATIONAL DISH: Chelow kebab, a meat dish with saffron rice and sumac spices

AMAZING!
Iranians value honoring others and showing humility. The Bible encourages us to do these things too! Philippians 2:3-4 says, "When you do things, do not let selfishness or pride be your guide. **Be humble and give more honor to others than to yourselves. Do not be interested only in your own life, but be interested in the lives of others**" (ICB).

INDIA

CHINA

IRAN

EXPLORE THE COUNTRY **Over 89 million people live in Iran, a country** that has history dating all the way back to 550 years before Jesus was born! It used to be called Persia, as it's called in the Bible. A lot of Iran is desert; however, there are also many gorgeous mountain ranges like the Elburz Mountains, where Iran's capital, Tehrān, sits at the base. Iran is situated between the Arabian Sea, the Caspian Sea, and countries like Afghanistan and Iraq.

PAKISTAN

PAKISTAN

EXPLORE THE COUNTRY
Pakistan is a country with a massive population of over 241 million people! The country is found near the Himalayas and on the coast of the Arabian Sea. Pakistan became a country during a time called the Partition when what was known as British India was split in two, India and Pakistan. Pakistan has diverse landscapes from mountains to plateaus, valleys, river plains, and beaches.

AFGHANISTAN

IRAN

MUNTJACS
This small deer known as the northern red muntjac is called the "barking deer" because it makes sounds like a dog barking.

Football (soccer) is incredibly important to Pakistanis, but not just as a pastime. **Pakistan manufactures 70% of the world's soccer balls**, and they created balls especially for the World Cup in 2022.

The Karakoram Highway is the highest international road ever built, and it runs 500 miles from Islamabad, Pakistan, to Kashgar, China! The highest point is called Khunjerab Pass, and it's 15,397 feet high.

GHARIALS
The gharial might be a subspecies of crocodile, but its long, narrow snout makes these guys easy to identify! The snout's unique shape allows the gharial to easily surprise and catch fish, their favorite food. Though once commonly found in Pakistan, they now have a small presence in the country. Pakistani officials are attempting to increase the gharial population and protect their habitat.

INDUS RIVER DOLPHINS
Pakistan is home to a species of dolphin that lives in rivers, not oceans, called the Indus river dolphin. However, their habitats are quickly disappearing, and Indus river dolphins have had to adapt to living in muddy rivers in which they can't see, using echolocation to guide them.

YELLOW-BELLIED SEA SNAKES
Yellow-bellied sea snakes live in the salty ocean, but they only drink fresh water. So how do they get fresh water? They drink rainwater from the surface of the sea!

ARABIAN SEA

The Tharparkar Desert is the only fertile desert in the world, which means that despite the lack of rain, lots of plants can grow there! You can find this unique ecosystem in the Sindh province.

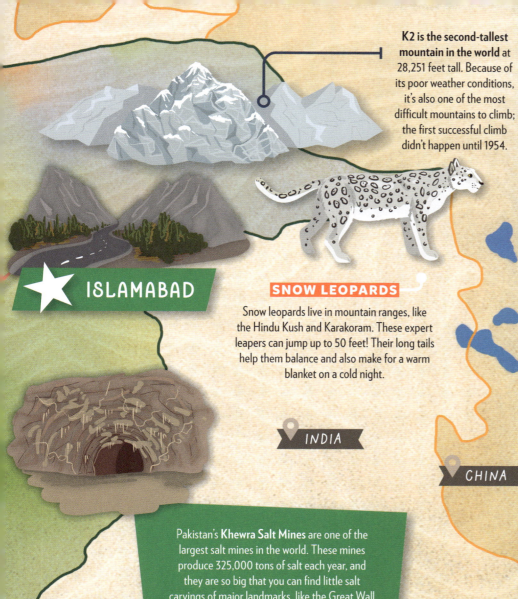

K2 is the second-tallest mountain in the world at 28,251 feet tall. Because of its poor weather conditions, it's also one of the most difficult mountains to climb; the first successful climb didn't happen until 1954.

★ ISLAMABAD

SNOW LEOPARDS
Snow leopards live in mountain ranges, like the Hindu Kush and Karakoram. These expert leapers can jump up to 50 feet! Their long tails help them balance and also make for a warm blanket on a cold night.

 INDIA

Pakistan's **Khewra Salt Mines** are one of the largest salt mines in the world. These mines produce 325,000 tons of salt each year, and they are so big that you can find little salt carvings of major landmarks, like the Great Wall of China, on the walls.

KEY FACTS

OFFICIAL LANGUAGES: English and Urdu

CAPITAL CITY: Islamabad

NEIGHBORING COUNTRIES & BODIES OF WATER: India, Arabian Sea, Iran, Afghanistan, China

NATIONAL TREE: Deodar cedar

NATIONAL FLOWER: Jasmine

NATIONAL BIRD: Chukar partridge

NATIONAL DISH: Nihari, which is a rich beef stew flavored with spices

 CHINA

SHAHBAZ BHATTI
LIFESPAN: September 9, 1968–March 2, 2011
BIRTHPLACE: Lahore, Pakistan

Shabaz was a politician and one of Pakistan's few Christians working in the government. Even though he received many death threats and was eventually killed, he fought tirelessly for religious freedoms for all and spoke out against religious persecution.

SAINT THOMAS THE APOSTLE
LIFESPAN: Unknown–c. AD 53
BIRTHPLACE: Galilee, Israel

Though many know him as "Doubting Thomas" because he struggled to believe Jesus rose from the dead, Thomas the Apostle is believed to be the person who first brought the gospel to the part of the world that is now known as Pakistan.

 NEPAL

Malala Yousafzai, a vocal supporter of free and safe education for girls, was a cowinner of the Nobel Peace Prize in 2014. The young Pakistani girl was only 17 at the time, making her the youngest Nobel laureate ever!

BE AN EXAMPLE
Malala gave her first speech about girls having the right to an education when she was only 11 years old. **First Timothy 4:12** tells us, "You are young, but do not let anyone treat you as if you were not important. Be an example to show the believers how they should live. Show them with your words, with the way you live, with your love, with your faith, and with your pure life" (ICB). It doesn't matter how old you are—God can still use you to do great things!

The Indian portion of the Himalayas is considered **tectonically active**, meaning the surface of the earth continues to shift and change. Because of this movement, India is subject to lots of earthquakes and landslides.

KEY FACTS

OFFICIAL LANGUAGES: Hindi and English

CAPITAL CITY: New Delhi

NEIGHBORING COUNTRIES & BODIES OF WATER: Pakistan, China, Nepal, Bhutan, Bangladesh, Myanmar, Bay of Bengal, Laccadive Sea, Arabian Sea, Indian Ocean

NATIONAL TREE: Banyan

NATIONAL FLOWER: Lotus

NATIONAL BIRD: Indian Peafowl

NATIONAL DISH: No official dish, but India is known for khichdi, a dish made of rice and lentils

CHINA

NEPAL

BHUTAN

MYANMAR

SLOTH BEARS
Sloth bears might have a bear-like face, but their habits are more like sloths, carrying their babies on their backs and eating mostly bugs.

BANGLADESH

AMAZING!
Diamonds are considered precious because they are rare and highly valued. But you are worth more than any diamond to God! If you ever feel ordinary or unimportant, you can remember Isaiah 43:4, **"You are precious to me . . . and I love you"** (ICB).

BAY OF BENGAL

India was the first country to mine diamonds when the shiny stone was discovered in the Krishna River Delta back in the fourth century BC. For 1,000 years after that discovery, if you wanted a diamond, you didn't go to a jewelry store—you went to India!

THAILAND

LAOS

CAMBODIA

If you love beaches, you'll love India! Because India is a peninsula (meaning it has water on three sides), a third of this country is made up of coastlines.

North Sentinel Island is one of the last "untouched" areas in the entire world. This means the people who live on the island don't have contact with the outside world or access to modern technology. To protect the Sentinelese people, no one is allowed to get within five nautical miles of the island.

INDIA

INDIAN OCEAN

EXPLORE THE COUNTRY
India is a massive country with over 1.4 billion people, including thousands of different ethnic groups and hundreds of languages spoken. It's not surprising that India is the most populous country. It is home to amazing architecture like the Taj Mahal, delicious foods, and truly stunning nature.

HIMALAYAS

The Himalayas are so massive that astronauts on the **International Space Station** have captured pictures of the mountain range!

The Himalayas cover **75% of Nepal**, and Nepalese people call Mount Everest "Sagarmatha," which can be translated as "peak of heaven."

Climbing Mount Everest is incredibly dangerous, so some Nepalese people serve as guides called Sherpas. An expert guide can show you the safe places to climb and keep you headed in the right direction. The Bible says we also have Someone who protects us and guides us. Psalm 23 tells us, **"The Lord is my shepherd. I have everything I need. . . . For the good of his name, he leads me on paths that are right"** (ICB). When we need help, God is our Shepherd, our very own expert guide.

OUR GUIDE

The Himalayas are the **third-largest collection of ice and snow** in the world after the Arctic and Antarctica. There are around **15,000 glaciers**, including the Siachen Glacier, the second-longest glacier outside of the North and South Poles.

Despite its name, the red panda isn't related to the giant panda, but they both enjoy snacking on bamboo! These adorable mammals also **love to nap**, spending two-thirds of their day snoozing, wrapped up in their own bushy tails for warmth.

The **Himalayan wild yak** might sound ferocious because of its name, but the locals consider them to be pretty tame and domesticated. These gentle giants can grow up to six feet tall at their shoulders.

EXPLORE THE ECOSYSTEM

The Himalayas are a massive mountain range that stretches through the countries of India, Pakistan, Afghanistan, China, Bhutan, and Nepal. This range is about 1,550 miles long, and it contains the tallest mountain in the entire world (above sea level), Mount Everest. These mountains have fascinated people for generations, and are regularly seen in South Asian literature, mythology, and art. The Himalayas are known for their high, jagged peaks (which makes climbing them extra challenging), massive glaciers, and deep gorges.

When global plate-tectonic forces moved the Earth's crust, the Himalayas formed. The Himalayas still have a lot of **tectonic plate movement** today, meaning there are many earthquakes and tremors.

Though their name might suggest otherwise, **Himalayan blue sheep** are neither blue nor sheep. These mammals live in the rocky regions of the Himalayas. When faced with a predator, these animals stand perfectly still, and their slate-gray coat helps them blend in with the rocks around them.

Snow and ice cover much of the Himalayas, but at lower elevations, you can find several types of forests (including some tropical ones!) as well as green plant life.

The **Himalayan monal pheasant** might have brilliantly colored feathers, but their most useful feature is their beak. These birds are expert diggers, using their beaks to dig for food like plants, roots, and bugs.

The Himalayas are a huge mountain range, yet Matthew 17:20 says that if we have faith in God, we'll be able to move mountains and **nothing will be impossible for us**. How big must God be if our faith in Him could enable us to do seemingly impossible things? Take a moment to thank God for how great He is!

Himalayan marmots live in big colonies, and they are **incredibly social and friendly** with other marmots in their community. They say hello with adorable nose-to-nose greetings, groom each other, and even wrestle as play!

CHINA

EXPLORE THE COUNTRY **China has the second-largest population in the entire world.** Over a billion people live there! China takes up nearly the entire eastern portion of the continent of Asia, with lots of mountain, desert, and tropical beach climates to enjoy. The varied climates make China the perfect home for some truly unique animals.

China is the **fourth-largest country** by land mass, but it has only one time zone!

KAZAKHSTAN

The biggest holiday in China is Chinese New Year, which is also called Lunar New Year because the festival begins each year with the first new moon that falls between January 21 and February 20. Celebrations last for 15 days and include fireworks, red clothing, and decorations.

KYRGYZSTAN

AMAZING!

The **Giant Panda Protection and Research Center** in the Sichuan province hires caring people to do nothing but play with pandas! Doesn't this sound like the best job in the world? Proverbs 12:10 says, "The righteous care for the needs of their animals" (NIV). You may not be able to move to China to babysit pandas, but you can help care for animals in your home, neighborhood, and community.

MONGOLIA

TAJIKISTAN

AFGHANISTAN

PAKISTAN

China is full of mountains, with a third of the country being mountain ranges! The tallest mountain on Earth, **Mount Everest**, is found on the border of China and Nepal.

GIANT PANDAS

Giant pandas are native to China and one of the rarest mammals on Earth. They spend around 10 to 16 hours of the day chowing down on their favorite snack, bamboo.

SICHUAN GOLDEN SNUB-NOSED MONKEYS

Sichuan golden snub-nosed monkeys live in trees high up in the mountains where there isn't as much oxygen. So in addition to their thick fur to keep them warm, they also have big nostrils and thick lips to help them take in as much oxygen as possible.

LEARN THE LANGUAGE

MANDARIN

Mandarin is the most commonly spoken form of Chinese. About a billion people speak this language worldwide! And instead of having an alphabet, Mandarin uses symbols that represent meanings, not sounds.

BHUTAN

INDIA

BANGLADESH

LONG-EARED JERBOAS

The long-eared jerboa is a small rodent with long ears, long hind legs, and a long tail. It can jump like a kangaroo!

VIETNAM

MYANMAR

LAOS

It's said that **tea was first discovered in China** as early as 2737 BC. Drinking tea and holding tea ceremonies are important activities in Chinese culture. Tea is meant to be appreciated, smelled, enjoyed, and shared.

RUSSIA

The **Palace Museum**, which holds one of the largest collections of Chinese artworks, is housed in the Forbidden City in China. This city was commissioned in 1406 and finished in 1420. At that time, commoners were not allowed inside, hence its name.

BEIJING

NORTH KOREA

SOUTH KOREA

The Great Wall of China is a massive wall that spreads across the country. It starts in the east in Shanhaiguan in Hebei province and goes west all the way to Jiayuguan in Gansu province, spanning over 13,000 miles long. It took over 2,000 years to build!

The **Bailong Elevator**, the world's tallest outdoor elevator, will take you 1,070 feet up into Zhangjiajie National Forest Park in the Hunan Province. The glass elevator offers amazing views of the park's sandstone pillars, which reach as high as 3,500 feet.

PACIFIC OCEAN

TAIWAN

In 2022, the **China National Space Administration** completed its own space station, called Tiangong. It's only the second permanently staffed space station in orbit, and it's roughly one-third the size of the International Space Station.

KEY FACTS

OFFICIAL LANGUAGE: Mandarin Chinese

CAPITAL CITY: Beijing

NEIGHBORING COUNTRIES & BODIES OF WATER: Afghanistan, Tajikistan, Kyrgyzstan, Kazakhstan, Mongolia, Russia, North Korea, Pacific Ocean, Vietnam, Laos, Myanmar, India, Bhutan, Nepal, and Pakistan

NATIONAL TREE: Ginkgo

NATIONAL FLOWER: Plum blossom

NATIONAL DISH: Peking duck, which is roast duck with vegetables

FORGIVENESS

God gives us a clean slate when we sin and ask Him for forgiveness. In fact, Psalm 103:12 says He takes our sin as far away from us as the east is from the west. That's even farther than the two ends of the Great Wall of China! Is there something you need to ask God forgiveness for?

DING LIMEI

LIFESPAN: October 2, 1871–September 22, 1936
BIRTHPLACE: Shandong, China

Ordained as a pastor in 1898, Ding preached the gospel to as many people as he could find. He was imprisoned for his faith in 1900, but after his release, he didn't stop preaching. In fact, he became more determined and set the goal of preaching the gospel to every province in China.

JEANETTE LI

LIFESPAN: 1899–1968
BIRTHPLACE: Dexing, China

Jeanette became a Christian as a child and found ways to preach the gospel wherever she could. She taught in a school run by the Chinese government to reach kids who hadn't heard of Jesus, and then became a full-time evangelist, working with hospitals, orphanages, and other relief centers to help those in need and also tell them about Jesus.

SOUTH KOREA

EXPLORE THE COUNTRY South Korea is a bustling country that's home to over 51 million people, and it's a hub of music, dance, and fashion. The country is full of big cities! South Korea's capital, Seoul, is home to almost 10 million people. A country full of natural wonders (like bamboo forests) and manmade wonders (like the N Seoul Tower), South Korea isn't a place to be missed!

KEY FACTS

OFFICIAL LANGUAGE: Korean

CAPITAL CITY: Seoul

NEIGHBORING COUNTRIES & BODIES OF WATER: North Korea, Sea of Japan, East China Sea, Yellow Sea

NATIONAL TREE: Korean red pine

NATIONAL BIRD: Korean magpie

NATIONAL DISH: Kimchi, pickled and fermented vegetables with a variety of sweet or spicy seasonings

CHOE SANG-RIM

LIFESPAN: November 17, 1888–March 6, 1945

BIRTHPLACE: Dongrae, South Korea

Choe was a priest and a vocal fighter for Korean independence. He refused to bow down to the Japanese government and did not worship the Japanese emperor instead of worshipping God. Unfortunately, he was arrested and died in prison, but his legacy still inspires Koreans generations after his death.

WOW! South Korea **sends many missionaries** around the world every year. It's one of the top missionary-sending countries in the world!

FUN FACT In South Korea, **Christmas is a day you spend with your friends or your significant other**. It's not a holiday in which people typically travel to visit family. However, the Lunar New Year is a major holiday, and it's common to travel home then to spend time with family.

LEARN THE LANGUAGE

KOREAN

The Korean alphabet is relatively new. The Korean people only began using it in the 15th century. But many linguists (people who study language) praise the Korean alphabet as one of the best writing systems in the world!

JEJU-DO

The highest peak in South Korea is **Mount Hallasan**. This extinct volcano is found on Jeju-do Island and is 6,398 feet above sea level.

The DMZ, or demilitarized zone, is no-man's-land between South Korea and North Korea where no one lives and there's no military activity. Because of this, it's become an unofficial nature preserve full of forests and wetlands that welcome migratory birds, fish, and mammals.

NORTH KOREA

The **N Seoul Tower** is one of the most popular tourist attractions in South Korea because of its amazing views of the country. But don't look down. This view is 777 feet up from the ground!

RESPECT

South Korea puts a lot of importance on respecting elders, which is something the Bible talks about too! **First Peter 5:5 tells younger people to honor their elders**, and Hebrews 13:17 says to obey your leaders.

SEA OF JAPAN

★ SEOUL

RACCOON DOGS

The raccoon dog looks like a mix of a raccoon and a dog, but it's actually not related to either. Instead, it's a part of the fox family. These little guys are excellent climbers and are one of two species of fox that climbs trees!

LONG-TAILED GORALS

Long-tailed gorals are part of the goat-antelope family. They live in small groups of two to five gorals, and they prefer high elevations, living in mountainous areas with cliffs and small crevices that humans and other animals can't access.

AHN CHANG HO

LIFESPAN: November 9, 1878– March 10, 1938

BIRTHPLACE: Pyongan province, Korea (modern-day North Korea)

Ahn was a Christian who fought hard for the independence of Korea when it was under Japanese rule. He believed strongly in helping Koreans build better lives. He started the Young Korean Academy and founded the Provisional Government of the Republic of Korea. He also is believed to be one of the authors of the South Korean national anthem.

In addition to the mainland, South Korea has over **3,000 islands**.

Danuri was South Korea's first mission to the Moon! The **Danuri spacecraft** launched on August 4, 2022, and it was sent to study the surface of the Moon to help South Korea's future lunar explorations.

CREVICE SALAMANDERS

The Korean crevice salamander doesn't have any lungs! Instead, it gets oxygen by breathing through its moist skin.

Around **380 species of birds** can be found in South Korea.

MANDARIN DUCKS

Mandarin ducks are known for their colorful feathers. Unlike most ducks, they tend to build their nests high in trees rather than on the ground near water.

YELLOW SEA

South Korea is an honorific society, which means they highly respect others, especially elders. In fact, it's rare to refer to people by their first name, instead referring to them by their title. (In the same way, you wouldn't call your parents by their first names and would instead use the title of "mom" or "dad".)

EAST CHINA SEA

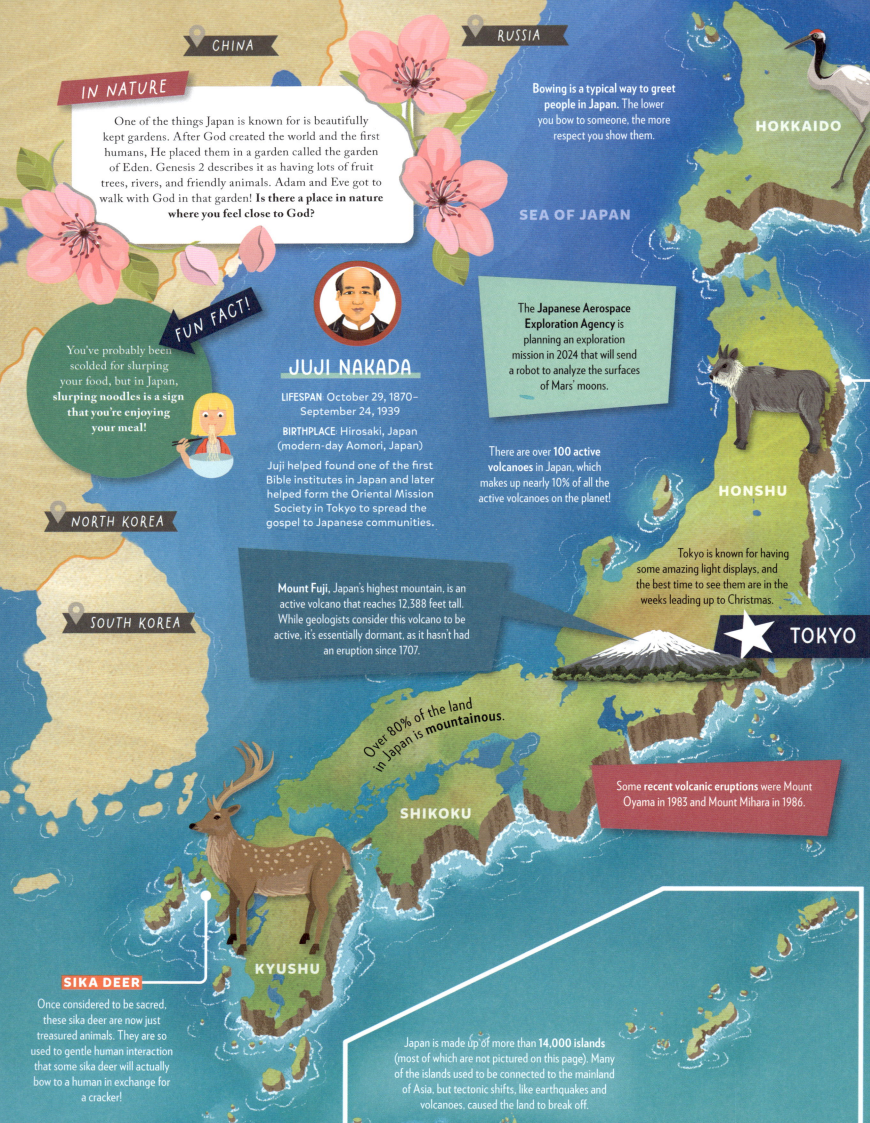

JAPAN

EXPLORE THE COUNTRY — **Japan is a string of islands between the Sea of Japan** and the Pacific Ocean with a population of 124 million people. Made up of four main islands—Hokkaido, Honshu, Shikoku, and Kyushu—as well as numerous smaller islands, Japan is a beautiful, mountainous country that is also a hub of technology and innovation. It's known for its distinct architecture, unique foods, and manicured gardens.

KEY FACTS

- **OFFICIAL LANGUAGE:** No official language, though Japanese is most widely spoken
- **CAPITAL CITY:** Tokyo
- **NEIGHBORING BODIES OF WATER:** Pacific Ocean, Sea of Japan, East China Sea
- **NATIONAL FLOWER:** Cherry blossom
- **NATIONAL BIRD:** Green pheasant
- **NATIONAL DISH:** Curry rice, a flavorful sauce served over rice

RED-CROWNED CRANES

Half of the population of endangered red-crowned cranes can be found in eastern Hokkaido, Japan. These cranes mate with one partner for life, and pairs are known to perform a ritual dance to strengthen their bond.

Japan is incredibly **geologically unstable**. The country gets up to 1,000 tremors annually, though they're usually small.

JAPANESE SEROWS

The Japanese serow, a goat-antelope with curved horns, is viewed as a national symbol by many in the country. Japanese serows are athletic, able to sprint and easily navigate cliffs. Japanese people, especially students taking tests, consider them a sign of good luck because they are confident, sturdy creatures.

IMAI YONE

LIFESPAN: 1897–1968
BIRTHPLACE: Mie, Japan

Imai was a Japanese Christian missionary who worked with a priest to help earthquake victims and even helped lead a nursing mission in Osaka. She later worked with *kamishibai* (street-performing) artists to draw Bible stories in this traditional Japanese style to help bring the Bible to life.

HUMILITY

The Japanese custom of bowing to pay someone respect is an idea echoed in the Bible. James 4:6 says that God opposes the proud and gives grace to the humble, meaning that **we please God when we aren't prideful and instead show humility to others**. Take a moment to pray and ask God to help you show humility.

Japan's most famous dish is sushi, which is rice with raw fish, vegetables, or eggs. The Pacific bluefin tuna is the most popular fish in Japan to use for this dish.

When you visit someone's home in Japan, it's **polite to remove your shoes** at the entrance.

PACIFIC OCEAN

LEARN THE LANGUAGE

JAPANESE

Japanese is known as the fastest-spoken language, with over seven syllables spoken in one second. That's like saying the following sentence in less than a second: God created everything!

KEY FACTS

OFFICIAL LANGUAGE: Vietnamese

CAPITAL CITY: Hanoi

NEIGHBORING COUNTRIES & BODIES OF WATER: China, Gulf of Tonkin, South China Sea, Gulf of Thailand, Cambodia, Laos

NATIONAL TREE: Buddha belly bamboo

NATIONAL BIRD: Tiger shrike

NATIONAL DISH: Pho (f-UH), a soup of broth, rice noodles, meat, and herbs

INDIA

BANGLADESH

One of the most common ways to get around Vietnam is via motorbike. You can find **over 7 million motorbikes** in Ho Chi Minh City and over 5 million in Hanoi!

NGUYỄN VĂN THUẬN

LIFESPAN: April 17, 1928–September 16, 2002
BIRTHPLACE: Huế, Vietnam

Nguyễn was a cardinal deacon in the Catholic church who was imprisoned for his faith. He used scraps of paper to smuggle encouraging notes and prayers to other Catholics in the community.

MYANMAR

INDIAN OCEAN

VIETNAM

FUN! Table tennis, also known as **ping pong**, is one of the most popular sports in Vietnam and throughout Asia. Many people enjoy playing just for fun, but it's also an Olympic sport!

EXPLORE THE COUNTRY **Vietnam is a richly diverse country filled with gorgeous rainforests**, thousands of rivers, as much delicious tropical fruit as you can eat, and 54 different ethnic groups among its 100 million residents. This S-shaped country has a tropical climate with plenty of rainfall, which means there is green as far as the eye can see and over 2,000 miles of beautiful coastline.

INDONESIA

MYANMAR • THAILAND • LAOS • VIETNAM • CAMBODIA

EXPLORE THE COUNTRY Indonesia is an archipelago (or a group of islands—**over 17,000**) in the Indian and Pacific Oceans. It's also the largest country in Southeast Asia, with a population of 278 million people! Formerly called the Dutch East Indies, Indonesia declared its independence from the Netherlands in 1945, though the Dutch didn't officially recognize its independence until 1949.

FAMILY!
Indonesians place a lot of importance on family relationships, but did you know we have a spiritual family in addition to our earthly family? Galatians 3:26–29 says that **we are all children of God through faith in Jesus**. In other words, fellow Christians are our brothers and sisters!

Lake Toba is the largest volcanic lake on Earth, and it's found on the island of Sumatra. It's over 1,600 feet deep and over 98,000 feet wide.

BRUNEI • MALAYSIA

ANOAS
The anoa is a small species of buffalo that looks similar to water buffalo. However, instead of curved horns, their horns are straight and stick out from the back of their head.

INDIAN OCEAN

With over **300 different ethnic groups** in Indonesia, you may experience a different type of Indonesian culture each time you visit.

The equator cuts through Indonesia and covers a distance that is one-eighth of the Earth's circumference.

ALBERTUS SOEGIJAPRANATA
LIFESPAN: November 25, 1896–July 22, 1963
BIRTHPLACE: Surakarta, Indonesia

Though he was born Muslim, Albertus converted to Catholicism and became the first Indonesian-born bishop, using his position to serve local Indonesians. When the country was invaded by Japanese soldiers in the early 1940s, he stood guard over his church and community, ultimately helping the Japanese troops call a truce with the local Indonesian community.

JAKARTA ★

Indonesia is the country with the most active volcanoes in the world. There are **127 active volcanoes** in Indonesia, with the most active being **Mount Merapi**, which erupts every two to three years!

The island of **Bali** is a popular vacation **destination** because of its gorgeous beaches, fun surfing spots, and beautiful scenery—like waterfalls and lush rice terraces, which are rice fields carved into mountains.

FUN FACT

Families are incredibly close in **Indonesia**, and it isn't typical for children to move out of their parents' home, even if they can financially afford the move. It's also not unusual to see extended family like aunts, grandparents, and uncles living under the same roof.

In 1976, Indonesia became the first developing country to conduct its own domestic **satellite system, called Palapa**. The Palapa series of satellites were launched to help with regional communications between the islands.

PHILIPPINES

There are over **700 languages and dialects spoken** in Indonesia.

CRESTED BLACK MACAQUES

The crested black macaque in Indonesia is a tourist's favorite animal to spot in the wild, and these rambunctious monkeys are known for getting into some shenanigans! One macaque took an adorable selfie of himself, and the picture resulted in a court battle to decide whether the monkey or the camera owner owned the rights to the photo. The ruling? The photo belongs to no one!

KEY FACTS

OFFICIAL LANGUAGE: Indonesian

CAPITAL CITY: Jakarta

NEIGHBORING COUNTRIES & BODIES OF WATER: Malaysia, Singapore, Timor-Leste, Papua New Guinea, Indian Ocean, Pacific Ocean

NATIONAL TREE: Teak

NATIONAL BIRD: Javan hawk-eagle

NATIONAL DISH: Nasi goreng, fried rice often served with a fried egg, meat, and vegetables

KOMODO DRAGONS

Indonesia is home to dragons! Komodo dragons, that is. These guys are the largest lizards in the entire world, weighing around 150 pounds. Indonesia is the only place on the planet where you can spot them in the wild!

Over 100 species of **endangered animals** live in Indonesia.

TIMOR-LESTE

PACIFIC OCEAN

Indonesia takes up only 1% of the land area of the globe, but the **Indonesian rainforests house a staggering amount of biodiversity.** You'll find 10% of the world's plant species, 12% of all mammal species, and 17% of all known bird species in Indonesian rainforests!

GOD'S TIMING!

Indonesians embrace an attitude of *jam karet*, which translates as "rubber time." This means there's no rush because time is flexible, and it's okay to do things at a slower pace. Have you ever wanted time to slow down? Perhaps you didn't want summer to end or to come home from vacation. The truth is, everything happens according to God's timing. Second Peter 3:8 reminds us, **"To the Lord one day is like a thousand years, and a thousand years is like one day"** (ICB). We just need to be patient and trust His timing.

Ever heard of the **Australian Outback**? It's the wilderness in the middle of Australia! Most people choose not to live there because it's so hot and dry. But God is always with His people, even in a scorching desert! Hosea 13:5 says that even when we're in the wilderness or burning heat, God cares for us.

Oceania is divided into four main parts: Australasia (which includes Australia and New Zealand), Melanesia, Micronesia, and Polynesia.

Not including Australia, over **14 million people** live on the islands of Oceania.

Australia and Papua New Guinea are known for having the **largest variety of marsupials**, or mammals who carry their babies in a pouch.

PAPUA NEW GUINEA

SOLOMON ISLANDS

FUN FACT! In 1932, Australia sent soldiers to declare war on its **national bird**, the emu, because there were too many of them—and they were messing up farms and crops. The wild part? The emus won!

The Dingo Fence in Australia is 3,488 miles long. It was designed to keep dingoes out of sheep-grazing areas.

Australia's **Trans-Australian Railway** has the longest section of straight track (so no turns or curves!) in the entire world.

The beautiful **Sydney Opera House** is visited by more than 10 million people each year!

AUSTRALIA

INDIAN OCEAN

Almost **90% of Australians** live along the coast because the climate in the middle is so hot and dry.

Australia is often called "**the land Down Under**" because the entire continent is south of the equator.

The biggest city in Oceania is **Sydney, Australia**. More than 5 million people live in Sydney, and more than 250 languages are spoken by Sydney residents!

Oceania is made up of people who live on thousands of islands, which means there is a lot of diversity. God's kingdom is also made up of people who have different traditions, but there's one thing that unites them: their love of Jesus! **Galatians 3:28** says, "You are all one in Christ Jesus" (NIV). That means no matter where someone is from, they're part of God's family!

Want to go for a drive? **The Great Ocean Road** is a beautiful route that runs along the southeast coast of Australia. It's dedicated to those who died during World War I and is the largest war memorial on Earth.

The **island of Tasmania** has some of the cleanest air in the world! There are walking trails everywhere, so you can leave your car at home if you need to go out and about.

MICRONESIA

MARSHALL ISLANDS

Nauru, a tiny island in Micronesia, is the only country in the world without a legally recognized capital city.

POLYNESIA

HAWAII (UNITED STATES)

PACIFIC OCEAN

Kiribati is the only country in the world you can find in **all four hemispheres**! Thanks to its many islands, the country spreads across the equator and the antimeridian.

KIRIBATI

MELANESIA

VANUATU

FIJI

SAMOA

AUSTRALIA
AND OCEANIA

NEW CALEDONIA

EXPLORE THE CONTINENT — **Did you know Australia is a country *and* a continent?** It's one of the smallest continents on Earth, but it's one of the largest countries on the planet! Australia is found in a region called Oceania, which has more than 10,000 islands in the Pacific Ocean that stretch between Asia and North and South America. About 45 million people live in Oceania, and each island has its own unique culture. Oceania is home to an incredible variety of wildlife, from wombats to birds of paradise to bearded dragons (a type of lizard).

NEW ZEALAND

The **Tasmanian devil**, found on the island of Tasmania, is named for its aggressive temper, sharp teeth, and fierce growls and screams.

People who are from New Zealand are often called **Kiwis**, named after the bird that's a symbol of the country.

Wellington, New Zealand, is the **southernmost capital city** on the planet.

Oceania is the **only home of the world's monotremes**, or mammals that lay eggs but nurse their babies with milk. Have you ever seen a platypus? That's a monotreme!

Temperatures can vary widely depending on where you are in Oceania. The hottest temperatures were recorded in the Australian Outback at a whopping 123 degrees Fahrenheit; the lowest were recorded in New Zealand at a chilly -14 degrees Fahrenheit!

Oceania is home to 14 countries: Australia, Micronesia, Fiji, Kiribati, Marshall Islands, Nauru, New Zealand, Palau, Papua New Guinea, Samoa, Solomon Islands, Tonga, Tuvalu, and Vanuatu.

Oceania's tallest mountain on land is found in New Zealand. **Mount Cook**, or **Aoraki**, is 12,316 feet tall.

INDIAN OCEAN

SAINT MARY HELEN MACKILLOP

LIFESPAN: January 15, 1842–August 8, 1909

BIRTHPLACE: Melbourne, Australia

Mary was a nun who provided free education to poor and Aborigine children. She also wasn't afraid to stand up to leaders even when it was hard. In 2010, she was made the first saint from Australia.

If you love looking at the stars, then head Down Under for some spectacular sights! With just a pair of binoculars, you can see the red dusting of stars known as the **Eta Carina Nebula**, right across from the Southern Cross constellation. And while you take in the awesome view, remember that God made every single star you see! Amos 5:8 says, "God is the one who made the star groups Pleiades and Orion" (ICB).

The song "**Waltzing Matilda**," considered the unofficial national anthem of Australia, tells the story of a man who is traveling the wilderness of Australia on foot, looking for work, and gets into some trouble along the way.

Uluru, also known as **Ayers Rock**, is a large stone made of tors (exposed, broken rock) in Central Australia. While Uluru stretches 2,831 feet above sea level, its massive rock slab also continues underground for several miles—like an iceberg made of rock.

KOOKABURRAS
Though the laughing kookaburra can't tell a joke, its call sounds like a loud belly laugh. Listen early in the morning or just after sunset to hear this "merry" bird.

Australia might be the **smallest continent on Earth**, but it's still about 372 miles wider than the moon!

KANGAROOS
A kangaroo's long feet and massive tail make it impossible for this giant marsupial to move backward!

DINGOES
You can find dingoes, the wild dogs that Australia is famous for, all over the continent. But if you really want to see one, visit the small island of K'gari. More than 150 dingoes live there!

About **80% of the wildlife** you'll find in the wilderness of Australia—like koalas and platypuses—are found only in Australia. That means you can see kangaroos in a zoo, but you'll stumble across a wild one only in Australia.

Even though Australia is known for its hot climate, the **Australian Alps** mountain range gets more snow than the Swiss Alps!

GOD IS OUR REFUGE
When joeys (baby kangaroos) are born, they're about the size of a jelly bean. So they live in a pouch on their mother's belly for six months until they're big enough to be on their own. We might not have a pouch to climb into, but in Psalm 9:9, **God said He's our safe space**. And not just for a few months. God is always our safe space!

GREAT AUSTRALIAN BIGHT

CANBERRA ★

The highest peak in Australia is **Mount Kosciuszko** at 7,310 feet tall.

BEARDED DRAGONS
The bearded dragon, found in Australia, has a spine-covered pouch that looks like, well, a beard! When this reptile feels threatened, its "beard" puffs out and turns black!

AUSTRALIA

FAITH
The most common **religion** in Australia is Christianity.

EXPLORE THE COUNTRY **Australia is a country filled with a mix of old and new.** For thousands of years, the native Aboriginal people have created a culture rich in art, using many forms of painting and sculpture. They even invented one of the coolest things ever: the boomerang! European settlers began to add their own traditions when they landed on the island in the 1700s, and today Australia is home to people with ancestors from all over the world. It's also home to some of the world's most famous landmarks, like the Great Barrier Reef and the Sydney Opera House.

PAPUA NEW GUINEA

PNG is only **436 miles** south of the equator.

FAITH
The vast majority of people from PNG identify as **Christian**.

INDONESIA

Mount Tavurvur is one of the most active volcanoes in PNG. Between 1994 and 2014, it erupted six times!

EXPLORE THE COUNTRY
Papua New Guinea (PNG) is an island nation made of two parts: the mainland and more than 600 smaller islands. PNG's mainland is located on the eastern half of an island called—wait for it—New Guinea! PNG shares New Guinea with its neighbor, Indonesia. PNG's 9 million residents enjoy gorgeous beaches, mountains, and at least 14 active volcanoes. And though PNG covers only 1% of the world's total land area, you can find 5% of the world's creatures living there—a huge feat for a tiny nation.

TREE KANGAROOS
Tree kangaroos are marsupials that are cousins to the kangaroo, but they are much smaller—around 30 pounds. They spend most of their time high up in trees in mountain forests.

AMAZING — Residents of PNG speak more than **850 languages**, and over **1,000 cultures** are found in the country.

★ **PORT MORESBY**

FAITH
About half of the people in New Zealand say they don't follow a religion, while **36% identify as Christian**.

Sky Tower, the tallest free-standing structure in the southern hemisphere, is found in the city of Auckland. At 1,076 feet tall, it's roughly the same height as the Eiffel Tower in Paris.

Sydney, Australia, is home to more than 100 beaches!

RĀWIRI TAIWHANGA
LIFESPAN: c. 1818–1884
BIRTHPLACE: Bay of Islands, New Zealand

Rāwiri was a tribal leader, farmer, and missionary who was one of the first influential Māoris to become a Christian. A quick learner and a good businessperson, he was considered the first commercial dairy farmer in New Zealand.

KIWIS
Did you know there are birds that can't fly? Meet New Zealand's most famous bird, the kiwi! It has feathers with a hairlike texture, and it doesn't have a tail.

New Zealand is full of volcanoes. There are **50 volcanoes** surrounding the city of Auckland alone!

TUATARAS
The tuatara is an ancient reptile that lived when dinosaurs roamed the Earth. Today you can find these lizard-like creatures, who love cool climates, only in New Zealand.

★ **WELLINGTON**

NEW ZEALAND

KEY FACTS

OFFICIAL LANGUAGES:
AUSTRALIA: None
NEW ZEALAND: English, Māori, New Zealand Sign Language
PAPUA NEW GUINEA: English, Hiri Motu, Tok Pisin

CAPITAL CITY:
AUSTRALIA: Canberra
NEW ZEALAND: Wellington
PAPUA NEW GUINEA: Port Moresby

NATIONAL TREE:
AUSTRALIA: Golden wattle
NEW ZEALAND: Silver fern
PAPUA NEW GUINEA: Earleaf acacia

EXPLORE THE COUNTRY
New Zealand—or as the native Māori (MOW-ri) people call it, Aotearoa (ow-tee-uh-ROH-ah)—is an island with just over 5 million people. It's located in the Pacific Ocean, about 1,000 miles southeast of its nearest neighbor, Australia. Do you have a favorite type of place in nature to explore? Chances are New Zealand has it. Gorgeous beaches, active volcanoes, icy glaciers, green rainforests, creepy caves, and gorgeous fjords—it's all here! And you'll find animals in New Zealand that you won't find anywhere else in the world, including Hector's dolphins and short-tailed bats.

GREAT

EXPLORE THE ECOSYSTEM

The Great Barrier Reef, found northeast of Australia, is the largest reef system in the world. About the size of Italy, this massive coral system is a huge (and beautiful!) ecosystem that's home to a wide range of fish and underwater plant life. The Great Barrier Reef is a 45-minute to two-hour boat ride away from shore, but this wonder of creation is worth the trip!

Did you know there are such things as **sea snakes**? (Bleh!) Well, if you visit the Great Barrier Reef, keep your eyes peeled for the 17 species that live there.

The **depth of the water** in the Great Barrier Reef varies greatly. In some parts the water is just over 100 feet deep. But if you go to the outer portions, the water can be over 6,500 feet—more than a mile—deep!

Just like the Great Barrier Reef needs algae to thrive, Christians need the Word of God to thrive. **Matthew 4:4** says, "A person does not live only by eating bread. But a person lives by everything the Lord says" (ICB). But how do we do that? By reading the Bible every day so that we can learn and remember His Word to help guide our lives.

Over 1,500 species of **tropical fish** live in the Great Barrier Reef. And 10% of all fish species in the entire world are found there!

If a coral reef turns bleach white, it's in big trouble! The white color means the water temperature or another stressor caused the coral to release its algae. If it goes too long without algae, the coral will die.

The **Crown of Thorns Seastar** is a marine organism that's no good for the Great Barrier Reef. It eats the coral polyps that make up the reef. Yikes!

Coral may look like a plant, but **it's actually an animal!** It's formed by tiny sea creatures called **polyps** that have a small, sac-like body and tentacles.

POLAR

The name *Arctic* comes from the Greek word *árktos*, which roughly translates to "bear." But this doesn't mean the animal! The name was likely referring to explorers using the North Star and the constellation Ursa Major (or the Great Bear) to navigate.

The Sun doesn't set in the North Pole for about **182 days** in the summer.

ARCTIC CIRCLE

UNITED STATES

RUSSIA

CANADA

Polar bears are found in the Arctic, but they aren't found in Antarctica.

The **Arctic Circle is an imaginary circle** that contains the land and water around the North Pole. Inside that circle you'll find the Arctic Ocean, of course, but also parts of Canada, Russia, the United States, Greenland, Norway, Finland, Sweden, and Iceland.

The Arctic is the **northernmost point** on Earth, while the Antarctic is the **southernmost point**.

The North and South Poles are **polar opposites**! The North Pole is mostly ocean surrounded by land, while the South Pole is mostly land surrounded by ocean. (And neither one has an actual metal pole to mark the location!)

GREENLAND

About **40 different ethnic groups** live in the Arctic region.

The island of **Svalbard** is part of Norway.

ARCTIC OCEAN

The Arctic Ocean might be the **smallest ocean** in the world, but it's still nearly twice the size of Australia.

ICELAND

NORWAY | SWEDEN | FINLAND

If you're hanging out in the **Arctic town of Longyearbyen**, don't be surprised to see reindeer casually walking along the streets. These reindeer are used to human interaction, and they're incredibly gentle, so they won't charge at or harm you.

YOU ARE A WITNESS

Jesus' last recorded words on Earth are in Acts 1:8: **"You will receive power when the Holy Spirit comes on you; and you will be my witnesses in Jerusalem, and in all Judea and Samaria, and to the ends of the earth"** (NIV). This means He wanted us to share what we've learned about Him with all people in all places—even faraway, remote places like Antarctica and the Arctic Circle!

Iceland has had over **30 glacial volcanic eruptions** in the past 200 years, but all that geothermal activity has created lots of natural hot springs to enjoy.

The Arctic and Antarctica are both cold, but **Antarctica is definitely colder!** Antarctica can get down to -128 degrees Fahrenheit, while the lowest temperature in the Arctic was -90 degrees Fahrenheit.

REGIONS

SOUTHERN OCEAN

The first child born in Antarctica was Emile Marco Palma, born in January 1978.

Antarctica is really far away from civilization and emergency doctors, so **scientists must pass extensive medical and dental screenings** before going. Some countries may even recommend or require that people remove their wisdom teeth or appendix in order to go!

About 30 different countries run around **80 research stations** in Antarctica. Between 1,000–4,000 researchers are scattered around the continent at any given time.

Vinson Massif is the highest point in Antarctica at 16,067 feet above sea level. It's also one of the "Seven Summits," which are the highest points on each of the seven continents.

Antarctica and the Arctic are both super cold, but **Antarctica is made entirely of ice**.

The 1958 Antarctic Treaty established Antarctica as a peaceful continent and a zone where researchers and scientists from all over the globe are welcome.

ANTARCTICA

Iceberg B-15, the **largest iceberg** from the polar regions, was bigger than the entire country of Jamaica, measuring 100,000 square kilometers. That's over 38,000 square miles!

Antarctica is known as the **highest continent on Earth** because it's average surface elevation is over 6,500 feet above sea level.

Antarctica might be beautiful, but **the climate is harsh**. It's the coldest, driest, and windiest continent on the entire planet. Winds have gotten up to speeds of 200 miles per hour.

One of the world's biggest mountain ranges, the **Gamburtsev Mountains**, stretches over 745 miles and has a peak that is a third of the height of Mount Everest.

ANTARCTIC CIRCLE

The dark days and harsh climates of the Arctic Circle and Antarctica make us appreciate the wonders of God's creation more than ever before. **Psalm 65:8** says, "They who dwell at the ends *of the earth* stand in awe of Your signs; You make the sunrise and the sunset shout for joy" (NASB).

EXPLORE THE REGIONS **Polar regions are the parts of Earth** that are found around the North and South Poles—the very top and bottom of the planet. These areas are extremely cold, so some parts have few human inhabitants. However, many explorers find their way to the polar regions, and their remoteness proves to be a great help for studying climate, space, and Earth sciences. And though there aren't many humans, some fascinating wildlife can be found there!

105

ANTARCTICA

SOUTHERN OCEAN

SNOW PETRELS
Snow petrels are small seabirds that are about the size of a penguin. However, even though their bodies are small, they are able to withstand the harsh Antarctic climates easily and can even live up to 20 years.

GENTOO PENGUINS
The Gentoo penguin is the fastest penguin on Earth, swimming at speeds up to 22 miles per hour!

WOW! Antarctica is the largest desert in the world—but it's not hot. **A desert is any place that gets less than 10 inches of rain per year**, and Antarctica definitely qualifies, getting around two inches each year.

Antarctica is the perfect place for astronomers, which is why the **South Pole Telescope** is found at the Amundsen-Scott Station. The high altitude and cold, dry air mean that the atmosphere is clearer, which allows for better study of the stars and galaxies.

Antarctica is the only continent without any **reptiles**. The cold climate would be too tough on cold-blooded creatures that rely on the environment around them to stay warm.

BLUE WHALES
Blue whales are the largest animal on the planet. Their whale songs are louder than a jet engine, and their hearts are the size of a small car!

Antarctica has **a waterfall that runs red**! Blood Falls looks ruddy thanks to iron-rich saltwater that turns red when it meets the air.

EXPLORE THE CONTINENT
Antarctica is the continent at the southernmost point of the world. It's the coldest and the windiest on Earth, so there aren't any cities, countries, or permanent residents living there. Instead, research bases are scattered across the continent so that scientists from all over the world can study the climate, wildlife, space, and more!

ELEPHANT SEALS

Elephant seals are the largest seals in the world, but their large size doesn't stop them from being expert divers. They can dive for up to 20 minutes and reach depths of 1,640 feet underwater before needing to come back up for air.

Flowers, trees, and bushes can't survive in Antarctica. **The only plant life** you'll find there are moss and algae.

AMAZING

Isaiah 40:31 says Christians find strength in Jesus and will soar on wings like eagles in hard times. Asking God for strength in a time when you feel worn out or weak can give you the same peace that a wandering albatross gets when gliding on Antarctic winds. So the next time you're feeling discouraged, **ask God for bravery and strength**.

Because of the Earth's tilt, Antarctica is in the dark all winter long, but in the summer, the Sun never sets. This means that **Antarctica gets more sunlight than the equator during the summer months**.

PENGUINS

Penguins have a gland in their beaks near their eyes that filters out the salt they ingest from eating ocean creatures. The gland traps the salt, which gets sneezed out of their bodies.

WANDERING ALBATROSSES

The wandering albatross has the longest wingspan of any bird on Earth—reaching over 11 feet long! They can fly for long distances without using much energy, as their giant wings help them glide on the Antarctic winds.

Antarctica is home to **90% of all the natural ice** on the entire planet and 70% of the world's fresh water.

Mount Erebus is the southernmost active volcano in the world. Despite the freezing temperatures, it has a "lava lake," which is a big pool of hot, liquid magma.

HELPING OTHERS

The Antarctic Treaty made Antarctica a peaceful continent for all nations to come and study the Earth together. **The Bible also talks about working together and helping each other.** First Timothy 6:18 says we are supposed to do good deeds, be generous, and be willing to share, much like the researchers do in Antarctica!

ARCTIC CIRCLE

EXPLORE THE ECOSYSTEM

The Arctic Circle is the northernmost point on the planet. Unlike Antarctica, the Arctic Circle has human inhabitants—about 4 million! Countries like Norway, Iceland, Russia, and more are partly within the Arctic Circle, and several Indigenous (or native) nations come from this area, like the Inuit, Yupik, Aleut, and Saami peoples. While it's not as harsh of a region as Antarctica, the Arctic Circle is still a very cold climate, especially the farther north you go!

The Arctic is home to about **20% of the world's fresh water**.

Walruses were created to thrive in the cold of the Arctic. When they swim in icy waters for long stretches of time, their heart rate slows down and their blood flow redirects to protect their brain and vital organs.

In the winter, a **reindeer's** hooves actually shrink to allow the reindeer to better grip icy or slippery surfaces! A reindeer can also see ultraviolet light that's reflected by the snow, which helps it spot predators more easily.

Winters in the **Arctic Circle** are cold and have very little, if any, sunlight. Summers have nonstop sunlight, and though it's still cold, the weather can get warm enough to have fog and rain in addition to snow.

Beluga whales are known for their vocal chirping, squeaking, and whistling sounds. However, they are also impressive mimics and are said to be able to mimic human voices.

Narwhals are unique underwater mammals known as "the unicorn of the sea" because of the long tusk on the front of their head. These tusks can grow to as long as nine feet tall! That's taller than an average-sized adult man.

INDEX

A

Africa, 36–37
Agnes of Bohemia, 64
agriculture, 35, 52, 69
Akrofi, Clement Anderson, 43
Algeria, 37
Antarctica, 104–107
Anthony of Egypt, Saint, 38
Anthony of Padua, 54
Arctic Circle, 73, 104–105, 108–109
Arethas, Saint, 79
Argentina, 34–35
armor of God, 32
art, 10, 27, 37, 42, 58, 59, 68
Asante, David, 42
Asia, 72–73
Australia, 98–101

B

Banting, Frederick, 10
Barnawi, Rayyanah, 79
Belgium, 52
Bhatti, Shahbaz, 83
birds, 11, 13, 17, 18, 19, 25, 26, 29, 31, 32–33, 35, 41, 45, 46, 54, 65, 66, 69, 71, 78, 87, 91, 92–93, 99, 100, 101, 106, 107
bodies of water, 11, 12, 13, 14, 16, 19, 21, 26, 33, 35, 37, 39, 41, 43, 45, 46, 49, 50, 56, 62, 66, 70, 72, 77, 78, 80, 96, 106
Bonhoeffer, Dietrich, 61
Botswana, 49
Brazil, 21, 28–29

C

Calvin, John, 58
camouflage, 95
Canada, 8, 10–11
Castillo Ramirez, Susana Paz, 24
caves, 8, 22, 37, 54, 64, 65, 66, 75, 95
celebrations/events, 25, 55, 65, 74
Chernobyl (Ukraine), 68
Chile, 21, 32–33
China, 88–89
climate, 8, 11, 21, 22, 32, 38, 39, 40, 41, 42, 45, 51, 58, 71, 77, 84, 95, 98, 99, 106, 109
Colombia, 22–23
Copernicus, Nicolaus, 64
coral, 102–103
Costa Rica, 16–17
Cristiani, Quirino, 35
Crowther, Samuel Ajayi, 45
Cuba, 18–19
Czechia, 64–65

D

dancing, 23, 24, 33, 45, 54, 66, 69
darkness, 11
deforestation, 31
Denmark, 53
deserts, 21, 22, 33, 39, 40–41, 48, 65, 79, 82, 106
diamonds, 85
disciples of Jesus, 27
Dulce, Irmã, 29

E

Egypt, 37, 38–39, 40
El Cid, 54
Elijah, 55, 79
Elizabeth of Hungary, 66
Esther, 81
Ethiopia, 37
Ethiopian eunuch, 37
Europe, 52–53

F

fear, 8, 95
fika, 63
Filipe, Luís, 54
Finland, 53
fishing, 27
forests, 12, 30–31, 45, 62, 64, 78. See also rainforests
forgiveness, 89
foundations, 14
France, 58
Frías, Juan de, 25
friendship, 57, 60

G

Gagarin, Yuri, 70
garden of Eden, 92
Germany, 60–61
Ghana, 42–43
glaciers, 35, 86
God, 13, 16, 25, 29, 31, 38, 39, 40, 47, 49, 73, 100, 103
Graham, Billy, 12
Great Barrier Reef, 102–103
Gutenberg Bible, 65

H

happiness, 45
harambee ("to pull together"), 47
harvesting, 69
heaven, 19, 50

Hidalgo y Costilla, Miguel, 14
hieroglyphics, 38
Ho, Ahn Chang, 91
Holy Spirit, 38
humility, 80, 81, 93
Hungary, 66
Hurtado Cruchaga, Alberto, 32

I

Iberians, 21
India, 84–85
indigenous peoples, 10, 12, 47, 48
Indonesia, 96–97
insects, 10, 14, 18, 23, 31, 43, 48, 73, 77
Iran, 80–81
Israel, 76–77
Italy, 52, 53, 59

J

jam karet ("rubber time"), 97
Japan, 92–93
Jesus, 14, 23, 24, 27, 40, 43, 57, 76, 78, 104
Jiménez, Jorge Volio, 16
John Paul II, Saint (pope), 65
Jordan, 78

K

Kenya, 46–47
King, Dr. Martin Luther, Jr., 13
Kiribati, 99

L

lakes. See bodies of water

landmarks/buildings, 8, 13, 24, 26–27, 29, 33, 38, 53, 55, 56, 57, 58, 59, 61, 62, 64, 67, 68, 70, 75, 77, 84, 89, 91, 98, 101
languages, 8, 10, 12, 14, 17, 18, 21, 22, 25, 26, 28, 33, 34, 35, 38, 41, 42, 45, 50, 52, 54, 56, 58, 63, 65, 66, 68, 70, 75, 76, 79, 84, 88, 90, 93, 95
The Last Supper (da Vinci), 59
Leonardo da Vinci, 59
Lesotho, 51
Lewis, C. S., 57
Li, Jeanette, 89
Limei, Ding, 89
literacy, 16, 34
Lloró, Colombia, 22
love, 13, 39, 53, 60, 103
Lwanga, Charles, 46

M

Mackillop, Saint Mary Helen, 100
Madagascar, 37
Makeba, Miriam, 50
mammals, 9, 10, 11, 12, 13, 14, 15, 16, 19, 20, 22, 24, 25, 26, 27, 28, 29, 30, 33, 34, 36, 39, 40, 41, 42, 43, 44, 45, 46–47, 48, 49, 50, 51, 54, 55, 56, 58, 59, 61, 62, 64, 66, 67, 68, 69, 70, 71, 73, 74, 75, 77, 79, 80, 81, 82, 83, 84, 85, 86, 87, 88, 91, 92–93, 95, 96–97, 98, 99, 100, 101, 104, 108, 109
Mandela, Nelson, 51
Martinez Garcia, Erelio, 18
Mary, mother of Jesus, 76
Mexico, 8, 14–15

monarchy, 52, 53
monotremes, 99
Montoya Upegui, Laura, 23
Mother Teresa of Calcutta, 84
Mount of Olives, 77
mountains/plateaus, 8–9, 10, 13, 14, 17, 19, 20, 21, 22, 25, 26, 28, 29, 37, 39, 46, 51, 52, 54, 56, 58, 59, 61, 64, 68, 70, 72, 75, 80, 83, 84–85, 86–87, 90, 92, 95, 96, 99, 100, 101, 105, 107
mummies, 33
music, 13, 15, 19, 23, 24, 45, 51, 54

N
Nakada, Juji, 92
Namibia, 48
national parks, 8, 12, 18, 42, 46, 51
Nauru, 99
Nepal, 86
Netherlands, 60–61
New Zealand, 99, 101
Nigeria, 44–45
Nilsson, Fredrik Olaus, 63
North America, 8–9
northern lights, 62, 108
North Pole, 104, 108
Norway, 62

O
Oceania, 98–99

P
Pakistan, 82–83
Papua New Guinea, 98, 101
Patagonia (Chile and Argentina), 34
Patrick, Saint, 57
Paul, the apostle, 74
peace, 43
Pelé, 28
penguins, 26, 35, 50, 62, 71, 106, 107
Peru, 26–27
pharaohs, 39
Philip, 37
plants/trees, 12, 14, 17, 18, 21, 22, 26, 30, 31, 34, 35, 36, 37, 38, 40, 41, 42, 44, 49, 50, 61, 62, 65, 68, 69, 70, 73, 77
plateau, 50
Poland, 64–65
polar regions, 104–107
Pool of Siloam, 23
Porres, Saint Martin de, 27
Portugal, 54
Prague, Czechia, 64
prayer, 16, 77
pyramids, 15, 37, 38

Q
quinceañera, 14

R
rainforests, 21, 26, 29, 30–31. *See also* forests
religions, 9, 10, 14, 17, 19, 22, 27, 42, 44, 46, 48, 51, 70, 101
reptiles/amphibians, 12, 14, 17, 19, 20, 25, 26, 30, 31, 33, 34, 35, 38, 42, 45, 56, 59, 68, 81, 82, 91, 95, 97, 100, 101, 102
respect, 91
rest, 63
Ring of Fire, 14
rivers. *See bodies of water*
roads, 35, 55, 61, 67, 82, 98
rock formations, 8, 10, 12, 15, 42, 45, 47, 48, 54, 67, 71, 78, 80, 100
Rome, Italy, 59
Romero Meneses, Sor Maria, 17
Roosevelt, Eleanor, 35
roots, 17
Rosario Brochero, Jose Gabriel del, 34
Rose of Lima, 27
Russia, 53, 70–71

S
sadness, 8
salt and light, 21
salt formations, 65, 83
Sambayi Oriedo, Esau Khamati, 47
Sang-rim, Choe, 90
Sapara Williams, Christopher Alexander, 45
Saudi Arabia, 79
savanna, 42, 45, 49
Scotland, 56
sea creatures, 11, 13, 14, 15, 18, 22, 25, 26, 35, 39, 43, 61, 82, 102, 103, 106, 107, 109
Sedarous, Hilana, 39
Seraphim of Sarov, 70
Siberia, 71
Singapore, 73
Singh, Bakht, 84
Skau Berntsen, Annie, 63
sleep, 55
Slovakia, 66
Soegijapranata, Albertus, 96
South Africa, 50–51
South America, 20–21
South Korea, 90–91
South Pole, 104
space, 30, 50, 56, 67
space/satellites, 11, 13, 22, 25, 26, 29, 33, 35, 41, 43, 44, 46, 47, 48, 50, 59, 61, 64, 67, 70, 74, 77, 84, 89, 91, 92, 97, 100, 108
Spain, 54–55
sports, 10, 19, 28, 29, 35, 36, 44, 57, 75, 82, 84, 94
strength, 107
subantarctic latitudes, 21
Sudan, 37
Suriname, 21
Sweden, 62–63
Switzerland, 60–61

T
Taiwhanga, Rāwiri, 101
Tamayo Méndez, Arnaldo, 18
Tasmania, 98
ten Boom, Corrie, 60
thankfulness, 58
Thomas, the apostle, 83
Toivo ya Toivo, Andimba, 49
Tolkien, J. R. R., 57
Türkiye (Turkey), 53, 74–75
Tutu, Desmond, 51

U
Uganda, 46
Ukraine, 68–69
United Kingdom, 56–57
United States, 12–13
University of Karueein (Morocco), 36–37

V
Văn Thuận, Nguyên, 94
Vatican City (Rome), 53
Venezuela, 24–25
Vespucci, Amerigo, 20
Vietnam, 94–95
Vladimir the Great, 69
volcanoes, 13, 14, 16, 22, 33, 37, 40, 59, 71, 92, 96, 101
Vylkove, Ukraine, 68

W
Wales, 56
water. *See bodies of water*
waterfalls, 8–9, 25, 35, 49, 61, 78, 80, 106
weaving, 27
worry, 8
Wurmbrand, Richard, 67

Y
Yone, Imai, 93
Yousafzai, Malala, 83

Z
Zapata, Emiliano, 15
Zimbabwe, 49

LOUIE GIGLIO is pastor of Passion City Church and the original visionary of the Passion movement. Since 1997, Passion Conferences has gathered over one million collegiate-aged young people in events across the US and around the world—all under the banner of leveraging their lives for what matters most. Louie is the national-bestselling author of over a dozen books, including *Don't Give the Enemy a Seat at Your Table*, *At the Table with Jesus*, *Goliath Must Fall*, *Indescribable: 100 Devotions About God and Science*, *The Comeback*, *The Air I Breathe*, *I Am Not but I Know I Am*, and others. As a communicator, Louie is widely known for messages such as "Indescribable" and "How Great Is Our God." An Atlanta native and graduate of Georgia State University, Louie has done postgraduate work at Baylor University and holds a master's degree from Southwestern Baptist Theological Seminary. Louie and his wife, Shelley, make their home in Atlanta.

NICOLA ANDERSON has been an illustrator and graphic designer since she could hold a crayon in her hand but has been working professionally since 2001. After many years working in the design industry, she now crafts imaginary worlds from her home studio, AndoTwin Studio, in Manchester, UK. During this time, she has worked with an eclectic range of clients and has loved every minute!

LYNSEY WILSON is an illustrator who works primarily in digital mediums. She uses a variety of contrasting styles, making her a highly versatile artist. She is passionately creative, from using inks and paper to working with fabrics to baking. Lynsey lives with her husband and two children and will often be found walking her beloved dog, Rufus, along the rain-swept forests, fields, and canals of North West England.

Indescribable Atlas Adventures

© 2024 Louie Giglio

Tommy Nelson, PO Box 141000, Nashville, TN 37214

All rights reserved. No portion of this book may be reproduced, stored in a retrieval system, or transmitted in any form or by any means—electronic, mechanical, photocopy, recording, scanning, or other—except for brief quotations in critical reviews or articles, without the prior written permission of the publisher.

Published in Nashville, Tennessee, by Tommy Nelson. Tommy Nelson is an imprint of Thomas Nelson. Thomas Nelson is a registered trademark of HarperCollins Christian Publishing, Inc.

Tommy Nelson titles may be purchased in bulk for educational, business, fund-raising, or sales promotional use. For information, please email SpecialMarkets@ThomasNelson.com.

Scripture quotations marked ICB are taken from the International Children's Bible®. Copyright © 1986, 1988, 1999, 2015 by Thomas Nelson. Used by permission. All rights reserved. Scripture quotations marked NASB are taken from the New American Standard Bible® (NASB). Copyright © 1960, 1962, 1963, 1968, 1971, 1972, 1973, 1975, 1977, 1995, 2020 by The Lockman Foundation. Used by permission. www.Lockman.org. Scripture quotations marked NIV are taken from the Holy Bible, New International Version®, NIV®. Copyright © 1973, 1978, 1984, 2011 by Biblica, Inc.® Used by permission of Zondervan. All rights reserved worldwide. www.zondervan.com. The "NIV" and "New International Version" are trademarks registered in the United States Patent and Trademark Office by Biblica, Inc.® Scripture quotations marked NLT are taken from the Holy Bible, New Living Translation. Copyright © 1996, 2004, 2015 by Tyndale House Foundation. Used by permission of Tyndale House Ministries, Carol Stream, Illinois 60188. All rights reserved.

Nelson Mandela quote on page 51 is from the following: Michael Trimmer, "Nelson Mandela and His Faith," *Christianity Today*, December 10, 2013, https://www.christiantoday.com/article/nelson.mandela.and.his.faith/34956.htm.

ISBN 978-1-4002-4613-7 (HC)

ISBN 978-1-4002-4616-8 (eBook)

Library of Congress Cataloging-in-Publication Data is on file.

Written by Louie Giglio

Illustrated by Nicola Anderson and Lynsey Wilson

Additional spot art on pages 10, 24, 54, 56, 58, 60, 62, 64, 66, 68, 70, 74, 76, 78, 80, 82, 84, 86, 88, 90, 92, 94, 96 by Cam Schuessler

Cover and interior design by Kathy Mitchell

Printed in Italy

24 25 26 27 28 RTLO 6 5 4 3 2 1

Mfr: RTLO / Milan, Italy / March 2024 / PO #12246207